PRAISE FOR *WHY DO YOU CALL ME GOOD?*

"In this difficult period we face, it is rare to find something that speaks so powerfully about our times and so clearly about our lives. This book courageously speaks out and challenges each of us to ask: *Can we find any real answer to the most important questions we must all face?* This is not something simple. It is not something which anyone can easily avoid or glibly tweet out some answer which solves it all. When faced with multiple trying situations in life, each generation must find their own answer to certain fundamentally life-changing questions: *Who am I? Do I know the truth about myself? Can I live with this truth? Can I die with it?* If someone else says something about you, will you think this about your life: *Why do you call me good?* This book, which may appeal to the reader as a modern take of John Bunyan's perennial classic *The Pilgrim's Progress*, is sorely needed now. It offers us a profound analysis of the human condition in today's contemporary society, and brings into line key truths about eternal reality by the Almighty God our maker."

—William "Winkie" Pratney, author of *Youth Aflame: A Manual for Discipleship*

"From time to time, if you are an avid reader, you're likely to encounter a book that challenges how you think, what you believe, and generally disrupts your status quo. Such is the case with "Why Do You Call Me Good?" The authors have done their diligence in researching the Scriptures and have provided an abundance of references which speak to their primary topic. That topic is the misunderstanding, and in some cases confusion, on the matter of measuring a person's "goodness" against what the Scriptures speak to regarding a person's eternal salvation. Undoubtedly, there are multitudes of people who fall into this category. The book, though not judgmental at its core, is likely to be perceived as such for the following reason. The present view within the Church on matters which draw the line between dark and light has been progressively weakened with the influence of culture over the past couple of decades, consequently erasing any line of distinction. While I understand the importance of the truth being presented in this book, my hope is that the Holy Spirit will help the reader to discover the journey which moves them from doing good to being great in Christ Jesus."

—Dan Hicks, senior associate pastor, The Church On The Way

""Why Do You Call Me Good?" is a very timely book in today's so called Post-Truth era, when everything is relative and highly subjective where moral issues are concerned. The book addresses the important subject of man's self-righteousness in contrast with the eternal principles of the laws of God as written in the bible. There are similar books exploring the same topic on self-righteousness, but this book presents the subject in a way that most people can relate to in day-to-day life and relationships. It is a very good resource material for pastors, teachers, and believers who desire to share God's kingdom values to their own spheres of influence in creative, refreshing ways. The authors have thoughtfully written the book to draw the attention of the many good and decent people about the reality of man's lostness and the need to find their way back to God. I encourage people particularly the young to read this book, as it points to a life that is truly rewarding and eternal in purpose. The Lord God spoke through the prophet Jeremiah, "Thus says the Lord: Stand by the roads and look, and ask for the ancient paths, where the good way is; and walk in it, and find rest for your souls. But they said, 'We will not walk in it.'"

(Jeremiah 6:16). The "ancient paths" mentioned here was taken from the Hebrew word "olam" which means "eternal principles" or "that which came from eternity." In our short sojourn on this earth, this is the key to a blessed life filled with peace or rest. May this wonderful book help many to find their path back to the eternally good God. God loves us and only wills the highest good for us as he said in Jeremiah 29:11, "For I know the plans I have for you, declares the Lord, plans for peace and not for evil, to give you a future and a hope.""

—DANIEL BALAIS, senior pastor, Christ, the Living Stone Fellowship

"Many well-meaning people engage in virtuous works out of a sense of moral duty and because doing so make them feel good. This book unravels a common albeit unintended consequence of how religious works or zeal prevent many from knowing the truth about God, and consequently about themselves. Supported by extensive scriptural verses and the authority of the word of God, the authors explain why religion without the heart-transforming knowledge of the love of God is vain. If our salvation can be gained through religiosity or good works, then Christ need not die on the cross for our sins (Galatians 2:21). Truth be told, salvation is a free gift made possible by the grace of God and received by faith in Christ. This book underscores how the message of the gospel can set man free from misguided beliefs and practices that so pervade our society today. To anyone seeking to have a vibrant relationship with the one true living God—the foundation and source of everything good—I recommend this book."

—WINSTON REYES, pastor, Reign Church (Every Nation PH)

Why Do You Call Me Good?

For Lesley, with my love in the Lord Jesus, Stella Tumagial 4/15/2023

Why Do You Call Me Good?

Understanding Goodness that Leads to Eternal Life

DORY B. ALONZO
STELLA S. TUMANGUIL

RESOURCE *Publications* • Eugene, Oregon

WHY DO YOU CALL ME GOOD?
Understanding Goodness that Leads to Eternal Life

Copyright © 2023 Teodora B. Alonzo and Stella S. Tumanguil. All rights reserved. Except for brief quotations in critical publications or reviews, no part of this book may be reproduced in any manner without prior written permission from the publisher. Write: Permissions, Wipf and Stock Publishers, 199 W. 8th Ave., Suite 3, Eugene, OR 97401.

Resource Publications
An Imprint of Wipf and Stock Publishers
199 W. 8th Ave., Suite 3
Eugene, OR 97401

www.wipfandstock.com

PAPERBACK ISBN: 978-1-6667-5532-9
HARDCOVER ISBN: 978-1-6667-5533-6
EBOOK ISBN: 978-1-6667-5534-3

01/09/23

All scripture quotations, unless otherwise marked, are from *The Holy Bible, English Standard Version*. Copyright © 2001 by CrosswayBibles, a publishing ministry of Good News Publishers. Used by permission. All rights reserved.

Scriptures marked (NKJV) are taken from the *New King James Version (NKJV)*: Scripture taken from the *New King James Version*®. Copyright © 1982 by Thomas Nelson, Inc. Used by permission. All rights reserved.

Contents

Preface — xi
Acknowledgments — xv
Introduction — xvii

PART I: THE STORY OF GOOD BUT LOST

Chapter 1: Lost in Religiosity	3
Chapter 2: Lost in Intelligence	6
Chapter 3: Lost in Generosity	9
Chapter 4: Lost in Compassion	12
Chapter 5: Lost in Righteousness	15
Chapter 6: Lost in Obedience	18
Chapter 7: Lost in Passion	21
Chapter 8: Lost in Sentimentality	24
Chapter 9: Lost in Rationalism	26
Chapter 10: Lost in Contrast with Confidante	30
Chapter 11: Lost in Compromises	35
Chapter 12: Lost in Devotion	38
Chapter 13: Lost in Offenses	40
Chapter 14: Lost in Brokenness	43
Chapter 15: Lost is Lost	46

Contents

PART II: THE MEASURE OF GOOD PEOPLE—WORLDLY PERSPECTIVE

Chapter 16: The Characteristics of Good People   51
Chapter 17: The Heart of Good Works   54

PART III: THE ATTRIBUTES OF A GOOD GOD—BIBLICAL PERSPECTIVE

Chapter 18: What God Says is Good   61
Chapter 19: Good Works that Lead to God   64
Chapter 20: The Key Attributes of God   67

PART IV: NO ONE IS GOOD, ALL HAVE SINNED

Chapter 21: The Sinful Nature of Man   79
Chapter 22: The Deceptive Philosophies of the World   83

PART V: THE FOLLY OF SELF-RIGHTEOUSNESS

Chapter 23: The Vanity of Man-Made Efforts to Holiness   103
Chapter 24: The Futility of Self-Righteousness to Salvation   106

PART VI: WHAT MUST GOOD PEOPLE DO TO HAVE ETERNAL LIFE

Chapter 25: The Consequence of Man's Fall   117
Chapter 26: The Compassion of God for the Lost   125
Chapter 27: Jesus, the Only Way   128
Chapter 28: The Path Toward God's Kingdom   137

Post-Script: Epilogue   140
Bibliography   143

Preface

The circumstance that revolved around our writing of this book was beyond ordinary. It was year 2020, when life as we know it grounded to a halt, as the world grappled with the pandemic caused by Covid-19. As co-authors, we each live in two different continents while collaborating on this book. We saw firsthand how the geographical divide did not matter to the unseen virus; it knew no boundaries—not physical, social, nor economic. All of us were upended by the abrupt change in the everyday routine of our lives. Millions passed away due to the sickness caused by the novel coronavirus, or its complications. We were heartbroken and diminished with every news of the passing of people we knew, personally or distant.

The difficult year that we collectively had squared us up with the reality of death. It made us ponder about our life, our soul, and our God. When confronted with a larger-than-life phenomenon, and told to protect ourselves against something that we could not even see, what do we do? When men and women in body bags were being buried in makeshift graves, unattended by family and friends who were barred to say their goodbyes, where do we turn?

We turn to the one true living God—sovereign over all, who alone knows the end from the beginning. Faced with the transience of life, we look to God in whose hands our life and death rest. We take the cue from Moses in the Old Testament Scripture, who constantly made intercessions for the Hebrew people, especially when God pronounced a judgment of pandemic proportions upon them. Because of their unbelief and persistent disobedience against God's expressed commands, God meted out a judicial decree, which you can read about in Scripture (Numbers 14; Hebrews 3). Everyone who came out of Egypt—who were not allowed to enter the Promised Land—died in the wilderness. Only Joshua, Caleb, and the younger generation under the age of twenty were spared. Think about it, bible scholars estimate that there were around two to three million predominantly Israelites who left Egypt during the Exodus. More than two-thirds of this population died in a span of forty years. Picture them marching and wandering in the wilderness, then add to it the weight of constant deaths, funerals, and grieving along the way.

No wonder Moses prayed, "So teach us to number our days that we may get a heart of wisdom" (Psalm 90:12). He reportedly prayed this toward the end of the forty years, after seeing the older generation of Israelites, including his own family, die in the wilderness. Like Moses, we need to ask the Lord to give us wisdom and help us prepare for the life to come after we die. For we too are marching along and wandering in this passing world.

The choices and decisions we make in our earthly lives have eternal consequences. Thankfully, God so loved us, he did not leave us on our own. He ordained the way for us to be reconciled with him. Today we have the benefit of retrospection, to examine and to learn from the recorded biblical accounts. We have the Holy Spirit and the written word of God to inform and teach us about God's saving work in the person of his son Jesus Messiah.

Our confidence in writing this book is grounded on the authority and inerrancy of God's word. It is to our benefit to get a clear, accurate understanding of who God is and what he did out of his great love for us, as taught in the bible. This book talks about the unsearchable depths that the triune God went through to redeem mankind from sin and secure the salvation of those who put their faith in God through Jesus Christ. The God of the bible is not only gracious and kind, but also flawless in wisdom and clarity; there is a purpose—a good, restorative purpose—in everything that he says and does. In this context, we encourage our readers to put their thinking caps on, while reading God's word that occupy the pages of this book. Look up the scripture verses for yourselves and prayerfully inquire of the mind of Christ. Scripture fuels our

Preface

aspiration to become clear-thinking believers, taking God at his word and believing that "every word of God proves true" (Proverbs 30:5), even if the present circumstance does not bear it. We pray it is the same for you.

In a special way, this book reaches out to the many who hear God's word but do not receive, who press on with life convinced that their souls are saved. We were once among this group of good people, who like hearing the gospel and studying the bible, yet whose hearts remain unperturbed by sin. It is possible for man to believe he is walking with God, yet the cares and affections of his heart are not set on things of God.

Finally, this book is not about taking a moral posture between who are good and who are lost, who are true believers and who are false. These matters are known between God and you alone, because only he can read what is in your heart. We invite and challenge each one who gets a hold of this book to contemplate inwards as you read; examine how the Scripture-based insights can best serve yourself, not your neighbor, co-worker, or friend. The object of this book is not to point fingers at anyone. The object is to point each of us to God and what he has remarkably done for us through his savior-son Jesus Christ.

It is incumbent for us to get a correct biblical understanding of how God sees us and what God did for us because he loves us. Do we really understand what the redeeming work that Christ accomplished on the cross means? Why did Christ have to come in mortal flesh, live a sinless life, and die a crushing, shameful death on the cross? Have we thought about the divine transaction that took place between God the Father and God the Son, as Jesus' body hang bloodied and broken on the cross? What difference does a resurrected Christ make to each of us? Why is it so hard for many of us to let go of our self-taught ways and depend wholly on Christ?

We must carefully consider the truth that we hold. Christ calls us to take his word seriously to heart, know the truth about sin, and follow him. There is no other more consequential leader we can trust and follow than him who says he is the way, the truth, and the life (John 14:6).

Acknowledgments

William "Winkie" Pratney
Pastor Dan Hicks
Bishop Daniel Balais
Pastor Winston Reyes
Juli Ana Sudario
Jun Turla

"I give thanks to my God always for you because of the grace of God that was given you in Christ Jesus, that in every way you were enriched in him in all speech and all knowledge—"

1 Corinthians 1:4–5

Introduction

The Lord Jesus, a masterful storyteller, once told this parable about the kingdom of God:

> "Again, the kingdom of heaven is like a net that was thrown into the sea and gathered fish of every kind. When it was full, men drew it ashore and sat down and sorted the good into containers but threw away the bad. So it will be at the end of the age. The angels will come out and separate the evil from the righteous and throw them into the fiery furnace. In that place there will be weeping and gnashing of teeth."
>
> Matthew 13:47–50

This parable was told at the time when the disciples reported back to Jesus the results of their ministerial assignments. After teaching his disciples and giving them authority to heal the afflicted, Jesus sent them out to minister to the Jews in villages and towns around Israel. Understanding the parable in this context, the net which was cast into the sea alludes to the preaching of the word of God to anyone in the world who cares to hear. When the net was hauled to land, the catch revealed fish of every kind, good and bad. Jesus said so shall it be at the end of time. The angels will come and there will be a separation between the good and bad.

Indeed, among those who profess to believe in God—some do openly, some secretly, some reluctantly, some do not really know the God they profess. Even within the church today, there is a mixed set of people—those converted in faith as well as the unconverted, the heart-faithful as well as the head-faith religious, the true as well as the false believers.

There will come a time when the good will be gathered and the worthless rejected, but not until the end. Who shall be counted among the good? What does it mean when you describe somebody to be good? Why do you call him good? Do certain benchmarks like family upbringing, education, accomplishments, charity works, friendliness, and likability make a person good? Is goodness measured by adherence to a faith or spiritual belief? Do hard work, decent living, self-reliance, and pious works make a good person? Can good works rectify transgressions and save the soul?

If we answer in the affirmative and assume that certain yardsticks make for good people, then many people in the world should qualify for heaven. By this reasoning, if we act kindly, decently, and generously toward others, regardless of and independent of God, we shall be saved. So long as we love our family, look after our neighbors and friends, observe the laws, and do our share to make things better around us, we do our souls well.

And what about the self-professed believers and followers of God, who started out with faith conviction, but lost their footing along the way? Scripture is replete with stories of men who started out well, full of the knowledge of God, but for some reason went off-track—men like King Saul who ended up taking his own life, and Demas who deserted the apostle Paul because he loved the world. Some encountered Jesus face to face, heard him speak, and saw him heal the sick and broken, yet ended up unchanged and unsaved—like Judas Iscariot, many of the Pharisees, and Pilate who decreed Jesus' death on the cross. On the other hand, there were men who were looked upon as pagans, outcasts, and sinners by the early Jewish society, but in the end got saved—like the Roman centurion, Zacchaeus the tax collector, and one of the thieves crucified with Jesus on the cross.

So, what do we make of all these, a mixture of characters some of whom the bible records to have perished away from God, and others assured of eternal life in heaven. To be sure, the workings of grace in the heart is unsearchable and known only to God. Let us be careful to think people are saved because of outward appearances

Introduction

and professions of faith; on the other hand, let us not discount the work of grace for those who stumble and are not yet as strong in faith. For as Proverbs 21:2 says, "Every way of a man is right in his own eyes, but the Lord weighs the heart."

What about you? Do you see yourself to be a good person? What do you love best? Wherein lies the affections of your heart? What do you suppose God will say when he looks at your heart?

The Parable of the Net ended with a consequential question put forth by the Lord:

> "Jesus said to them, 'Have you understood all these things?'"
>
> Matthew 13:51 (NKJV)

Our eternal life and death depend on our answer to this question. Scripture says we are altogether going about life in the world today, good and bad. Yet one day there is sure to be a separation. The Lord paints it clear that we may be inside the net, and found worthless and thrown out, because we are not in Christ.

Let us take time to understand this matter concerning our soul—what does it mean to belong to Christ? Let us live today, mindful, that time will come when we shall face our creator God and be accountable to him, "And there is no creature hidden from His sight, but all things are naked and open to the eyes of Him to whom we must give account" (Hebrews 4:13, NKJV).

Let us look to the word of God to help us understand the truths concerning these things. Let us begin with the story of a character we call Lost. Let us examine her life, her pursuits, her words, what she values most, what choices she makes. Consider how she lives while inside the net, and see whether at the last day, she will be counted as good or thrown away as worthless.

PART I

The Story of Good but Lost

There was this nice young woman who lived in an upscale neighborhood and was known for her impressive accomplishments, generous acts, and good deeds. She was esteemed by the people around her as somebody who is confident and strong, yet approachable and kind. She lived a happy, content life with her adoring family and supportive circle of friends and associates.

Then came a season in her life when the wind shifted. It felt like she lost grip and her life spiraled out of control. Things started to go wrong one after the other until that tragic accident.

By the way, her name was Lost. Curious? Wonder why such a good woman bore that moniker. Good but Lost.

Who was Lost? What was her story? Let's find out.

CHAPTER 1

Lost in Religiosity

Lost came from a deeply religious family. She was raised by her devout parents, Mom and Dad Traditionalist. They observed major holy holidays, attended prayer meetings, and joined pilgrimage tours whenever their schedules allowed. They made time to participate in fund-raising events, donating generously to their favorite causes and charities.

The Traditionalists regularly attended Sunday church; however, they never really developed close friends from church. Occasionally, when they could not get in time for start of church service, they make sure to arrive in time for Communion. They never failed to give in the offering basket. Since they found no reason to linger for coffee fellowship chat with the other parishioners after the service, they usually left immediately for lunch.

Always excited what restaurant to try each time, the Traditionalist family enjoyed good food. Sunday after church was their family bonding time. Along the way, whenever Lost saw a homeless person in need, she is struck with pity and if possible hands out whatever available food or extra money she has.

SCENE 1. THE GOSSIP ABOUT A RELATIVE

[One Sunday after church, Lost and her family went out for a lunch meet with some close relatives in an Italian restaurant.]

Part I: The Story of Good but Lost

Lost: Hi Uncle Flatterer, Aunt Gossiper! So nice to see you.

Mom and Dad Traditionalist: Okay, so what would be good for lunch?

Aunt Gossiper: Hey, did you know that Scholar failed the board exams? Serves her parents right for being high hat.

Mom Traditionalist: Oh really? I just talked to Scholar's parents a few days ago. They talked repeatedly and proudly about how their daughter is poised to do medical residency training in a top-notch university hospital, not knowing that Scholar would be such an embarrassment.

Dad Traditionalist: Well, I guess money and connections did it for them, but Scholar wasted it.

Aunt Gossiper: What a shame!

Uncle Flatterer: Hey Lost, you're still the best. None of your cousins could beat you. Thank God, you're still the brightest among your peers. I still remember how ecstatic the family was when news broke that you got accepted in an exclusive university which offered the accelerated direct-entry BS/MD medical program. This allowed you to complete your degree in Medicine in just six years. Then right after graduation, you took the Medical Licensure exam and managed to land in the top ten. And look at you now with a successful career in healthcare at such a young age.

Lost: Thanks Uncle, those were tough years and I'm glad I made it on my own. But poor Scholar, I wouldn't dream of failing like her. I wouldn't be able to handle the pressure and shame. Thank you, Lord, for sparing me this kind of humiliation. I guess Scholar should study harder, double her efforts, and muster all her strength to bounce back. When she succeeds, then she can be proud to have done it because of self-determination and drive. Success, she should owe it to herself alone, not connections.

Aunt Gossiper: By the way Lost, don't forget the bible study on Wednesday. We will host it. I believe you were assigned to bring pasta and chicken barbecue for the fellowship meal after the bible study.

Lost: Oh yes, I won't miss it. I already placed the food order in advance. I hope and pray more people will join us.

Lost in Religiosity

Mom Traditionalist: Let's pray though that Mr. Liberal would not come because we really don't see eye to eye with his progressive mindset. Same with Ms. Conservative who is too much of a prude for me.

[Meanwhile, seated at the corner table were former students who went to the same university as Lost. They couldn't help but overhear the conversations going on among the Traditionalist family.]

Doubter: Back in college, I knew Lost was popular for her brains and good upbringing, but I didn't see her as the friendly social type.

Basher: Sure, she was not friendly at all. I guess it was because she was very competitive in class. Well, look what kind of family she was raised into. For all their religiosity, I think Lost and her family are a bunch of egotistical frauds. From the moment they sat down, they gossiped about that girl Scholar for her epic failure. And they were talking about bible studies and fellowship meals. Wow!

Doubter: Oh yes, looking so pious at church but living differently outside of it; hypocrites, right?

> "If anyone thinks he is religious and does not bridle his tongue but deceives his heart, this person's religion is worthless."
>
> James 1:26

CHAPTER 2

Lost in Intelligence

Lost began talking as early as seven months old. At age five, she was already getting the attention of the teachers at the prestigious A1Kids Montessori Center. She was a consistent scholar and A-student from grade school to college. No doubt, Lost was a role model. She was very popular in the campus for her wit and intelligence; however, she only had a handful of close friends. Outwardly, Lost was helpful to her schoolmates. She even let her high school seatmates copy one or two answers from her answer sheet during exams. After school though, she shut everybody behind. She didn't really care for the company of others, except for her high school best friends, Confidante and Merrymaker.

Even when she started attending college, Lost made sure to keep in touch with her high school buddies. Lost usually speaks with Confidante to get things off her chest when upset or troubled. Her secrets were safe with Confidante. She always found wise counsel from her friend. On the other hand, whenever Lost felt worn out or exhausted from her college studies, Merrymaker was her go-to-friend to unwind and have fun. They usually went to sing-along bars or bistros. The two girls were socially drinking and smoking when chilling in these cool, fun places.

SCENE 2. THE BETRAYAL OF A FRIEND

[After Sunday lunch with her family, Lost usually joined her friend, Confidante, for an afternoon iced coffee drink. This time, it wasn't just the usual friendly chat. Lost needed to unload something that weighed her down for the past weeks.]

Confidante: So how are you girl, anxiety written all over your face? Come on, spill it.

Lost: I'm so angry right now. I heard this strange rumor from Busybody, claiming that Merrymaker was spreading this fake news about me during our last high school batch homecoming. Good thing I skipped that event. Merrymaker apparently told many of our batch mates that I secretly flirted with Professor Hunk back then to pull up my grades in some subject, so I could qualify for the Valedictorian honors at our high school graduation.

Confidante: What? How could that be when you didn't even have a boyfriend in high school? Even during college, you made sure to set boundaries for men who wanted to date you. Why would Merrymaker say that after all these years? Wasn't she a close friend? No question you deserved that award. Though you cheated a couple of times, they were just minor. I saw how hard you worked to maintain your GPA. You had time for fun alright, but you never slackened in your studies.

Lost: I know. Professor Hunk was sort of extra attentive to me, but I didn't put any malice in that. Yes, sometimes we ate together in the school cafeteria, but we always discussed about schoolwork. I respected him. I worked hard for my academic achievements. How dare her slander me like that. She was just one dumb girl after all.

Confidante: Hey, girl, take it easy. Did you confront Merrymaker about this?

Lost: No, I refuse to dignify her kind. She made herself the life of the party at my expense. We had good times together outside school. Yeah, we did party with some random boys, but it was all clean fun. In school, I didn't really mingle, not with classmates nor with our teachers. I didn't trust people in general. You know that Confidante, right? That's why Merrymaker was such a disappointment. I let her into my world, but she betrayed me.

Part I: The Story of Good but Lost

Confidante: Well, could you just forget about her? I guess Merrymaker was not really your friend. She was probably envious because you were well-off, smart, and popular, yet you still managed to have fun outside school. Merrymaker was so out of your league, a shameless freeloader friend.

Lost: Exactly right, what a loser. I couldn't believe I spent a lot of sisterhood fun with that backstabbing social climber. To think I always paid the tab for all those hangout sprees with her back then.

Confidante: By the way, how is it going with the fundraiser event Music Therapy for Dementia Patients that you're organizing? Just focus on your good works and the Lord will bless all your efforts.

Lost: I'm praying for its success, but there's another story in this committee. Another headache!

Confidante: Oh dear!

> "The discretion of a man makes him slow to anger,
> And his glory is to overlook a transgression."
> Proverbs 19:11 (NKJV)

CHAPTER 3

Lost in Generosity

Lost was already a cheerful giver early on when she was young. Whenever her cousins visited for playtime, she always gave away even her most expensive toys. She often shared her packed lunch or bag of chips and sandwiches with classmates. Her parents made sure she celebrated her birthdays in school with extravagant food and tokens for everyone. Lost also gave nice and thoughtful gifts to her teachers on special occasions. That was why her teachers were extra fond of her. During holiday celebrations with family, she made sure everybody always got the perfect gift. Lost believed that pricey things make people feel more appreciated, and she beamed with joy whenever people acknowledged her generosity and her gifts.

SCENE 3. THE PUBLICITY OF CHARITY WORKS

[After unburdening her concerns to Confidante, Lost headed to the fundraiser event venue for ocular inspection. Lost discussed the details with Scrimper, the event planner.]

Lost: This place is perfect. But what about this thing I heard that you slashed the budget allocation on promotions and ads for the event?

Scrimper: Actually, this idea came from the members of your organizing committee during one of our meetings. The majority thought it wise to reduce promotional costs to offset the pricey five-star hotel venue for the event. For me, it made sense.

Lost: Well, as Committee Chairperson, I beg to disagree. Publicity has always been paramount in all the previous charity projects that I've organized and successfully staged. The stakeholders and healthcare beneficiaries had nothing to say but praises for the donors and me. The photo ops, press releases, news features, ads in print and social media attracted more donors.

Scrimper: Considering the economic downturn, your colleagues saw the need to scale down on some expense items like publicity cost. The estimated savings on reduced promotions cost would be added to the coffer of the beneficiaries. After all, this is a charity event.

Lost: The final decision rests on me. We will discuss this with the committee in our meeting tonight. I'm willing to shell out my own money to cover the total cost involved for promotions, if needed.

> "Take heed that you do not do your charitable deeds before men, to be seen by them. Otherwise you have no reward from your Father in heaven."
>
> Matthew 6:1 (NKJV)

SCENE 4. THE HARSH REBUKE

[After the meeting with Scrimper, Lost proceeded towards the exit and bumped into a familiar face.]

Taker: Hi Lost! Fancy meeting you here. How are you? What's up?

Lost: Hi Taker! Nice to see you, it has been a while. I'm doing well, busy with my charity thing.

Taker: Oh, as always, you're still the lady with a big heart. I am forever grateful to you for co-financing our NGO (non-governmental organization) project for clean green environment during its initial launch. It has been running smoothly since.

Lost: Good to hear. By the way, would you be willing to help a new NGO that's starting up in my hometown?

Taker: I'm so sorry, but we are terribly busy for the rest of the year. I have no extra hand to send to that NGO by this time. Perhaps next year.

Lost: Isn't it funny? I've given you huge financial help for the successful launch of your NGO project back then, and now you couldn't even return the favor. Here you are, thanking me profusely for assisting, yet you're turning your back on another NGO in need. You're a big letdown. I now regret helping you.

[Visibly irked, Lost left hurriedly. Taker was dumbfounded. He turned to his colleague to explain himself.]

Taker: Gosh, I didn't expect that. I never said I wouldn't do it. I just honestly explained my predicament because our hands are full until year-end.

Sympathizer: I thought she was all nice based on your comments about her before. What a harsh reproach and condemnation. She was certainly unreasonable. You didn't deserve it.

> "And though I bestow all my goods to feed the poor, and though I give my body to be burned, but have not love, it profits me nothing."
>
> 1 Corinthians 13:3 (NKJV)

CHAPTER 4

Lost in Compassion

Lost was adored by her loving parents. They treated her like a princess and were overly protective of her as an only child. When Lost was growing up in her teenage years, she developed a compassion for the underprivileged who couldn't afford to be hospitalized when they get sick. This inspired Lost to pursue a medical degree, to somehow fulfill that longing to help the less fortunate. She thought about being a traveling doctor to remote villages, and at the same time work in a prestigious private hospital. Helping the needy made her feel good deep inside.

SCENE 5. THE RULE OF AN AUTOCRATIC MANAGER

[Lost woke up to a new day refreshed and recharged. She was all set to lead a team of volunteer resident doctors, nurses, and church workers to a medical mission in a depressed area in a far-flung town, a long drive from the city.]

Undependable: Dr. Lost, we already loaded the boxes of medicines in the truck van. Shortly, the food supplier of vegetable porridge, sandwiches, fruits, and canned drinks will be here as well.

Lost: What? I thought the delivery time was five o'clock in the morning. We're supposed to leave by six o'clock, to reach the mission place by eight this morning. We sure are running late.

Undependable: I'm sorry, Dr. Lost. I forgot that the departure time was moved an hour earlier. I got busy last night tutoring my first grader son for his test and taking care of my mother who was feeling sick. I failed to notify the food supplier to make an earlier delivery.

Lost: This is an important mission for the poor and sick, Miss Undependable. I wonder where your heart is. One thing sure, your mind is not with us in this team project. Pull yourself together for now. How can I rely on you in the future? If you cannot prioritize our outreach missions, then it's probably better if you don't join us at all.

Understanding: Dr. Lost, may I say something? I know Undependable personally. She really cares a lot about participating in medical missions. However, sometimes it just becomes difficult to balance family responsibilities and the desire to serve.

Lost: I get that, but in the process, she becomes unreliable and risks becoming a liability to our mission trips. So, it may be better for all concerned if she just focused on the needs of her family.

Undependable: Dr. Lost, the food supplier just arrived. They are already loading the food in the other truck. In ten minutes, we're ready to go.

Lost: It's about time. Call all the volunteer staff so we can pray for God to be with us in this important mission.

[After praying, the team sped away. Upon reaching the destination, the team set up the welfare food station, the consultation tables, and the treatment tables. Right on time, by eight in the morning the team was ready to receive the village folks. By five o'clock that afternoon, Dr. Lost treated the last patient. The team successfully wrapped up the medical outreach and they headed back to the city.]

Lost: I'm proud of all of you. We achieved our task to feed and heal the folks who were in need in that remote town. Except for a minor setback earlier, everybody contributed to the success of our outreach project. We all deserve a pat on the back. I will treat you all to a sumptuous lunch tomorrow. So go home and rest. God bless you all.

Part I: The Story of Good but Lost

[Understanding and Undependable left together. Understanding tried to comfort Undependable over the earlier misunderstanding with Dr. Lost.]

Understanding: I tried to explain your situation to Dr. Lost. I'm sorry that she still made you choose between your family and the mission trips.

Undependable: I know, but it's alright. I thought it ironic though that somebody with a heart for the poor like her, lacked consideration and compassion toward volunteers like me. I too love to help, but I cannot set aside the needs of my own family while volunteering.

Understanding: You're not alone in that thought. Some of the staff I talked to also said the same thing about Dr. Lost. She is a good manager but lacks tolerance and goodwill to people who do not measure up to her standards and expectations.

> "Be kind to one another, tenderhearted, forgiving one another, as God in Christ forgave you."
>
> Ephesians 4:32

CHAPTER 5

Lost in Righteousness

Lost was taught and raised to be a good person, having been brought up by responsible, educated, hardworking, and devout parents. She attended Catechism classes for many years while growing up. She knew the Ten Commandments by heart and did her best to obey them all. Lost always gave her best efforts to doing the right thing, even as a child.

Mom and Dad Traditionalist were never called in by the School Principal or College Dean for any misdemeanor or behavior issues while Lost was a student. Lost was looked upon as a role model in school by many teachers and students.

SCENE 6. DISHONESTY IN SMALL MATTERS

[The day after the medical outreach, Lost set off early to her hospital workplace for the morning rounds with her patients. Afterwards, she proceeded to a popular seafood restaurant to celebrate with her medical outreach volunteer staff as promised. After Lost settled the bill, she requested Understanding to help her shop for a gift.]

Lost: I arranged a surprise birthday party for Confidante, my best friend. Help me find a gift for her, something unique.

Understanding: May I know what her interests are? Passions?

Lost: Actually, Confidante is a low maintenance person. She is happy with simple things. But of course, I will not give her that. It

Part I: The Story of Good but Lost

must be something fancy, practical, and useful, no matter the cost. She is my good friend after all.

Understanding: Okay Doc. Let's browse the electronics section.

Lost: Hold on, let me first check the credit cards I have in my purse. Got it, let's get going.

[Seeing a piece of paper that fell on the floor, Understanding picked it up and noticed that it was the restaurant lunch receipt payment made by Lost. Curious, Understanding went over the receipt and discovered that the additional items they ordered were not included in the itemized bill.]

Understanding: Excuse me, Doc. You dropped the restaurant receipt. I'm sorry I got curious; I looked over the order items listed in the receipt. The restaurant was shortchanged because the tab did not include the extra items we ordered.

Lost: Really? Oh well, they must have given those extra stuff as compliments since we were a big group. Don't worry about it. I'm sure if they made a mistake, they would bring it to my attention. I'm a regular at that restaurant. Come on, we're running late. Let's find that special gift.

Understanding: Do you think so? Well, as for the gift, how about buying her the latest smart phone, the most popular one in the market today.

Lost: Perfect. Let's grab it. I'm sure Confidante will be thrilled.

[Upon reaching the store, they purchased the latest smart phone model as planned and settled the bill at the sales counter.]

Sales Associate: You're lucky, this is the last stock we have on this very popular model. Is this a gift for someone? Would you like to have it specially wrapped for a reasonable fee?

Lost: Please do.

[The salesperson proceeded to scan the barcode for the smart phone and had the special gift wrap done. She handed the shopping bag containing the gift item and receipt to the customer, not knowing that she forgot to charge the special gift wrap fee.]

Understanding: I will receive the item for her. She's on the phone right now.

Lost in Righteousness

[When Understanding caught up with Lost, she handed her the gift package.]

Lost: Hurry up, I will be late for my other appointment.

[Lost drove away and dropped off Understanding at the bus stop. She stopped by a gas station for a refill. While waiting, Lost checked out the wrapped birthday present. She got hold of the receipt and noticed that the special gift wrap fee was missing.]

Lost: Oh gosh, not again. But I don't have time to go back. It's the cashier's fault anyway. I'll just do it some other time.

[Lost never returned to the store to rectify the underpaid receipt due to her busy schedule.]

> "One who is faithful in very little is also faithful in much, and one who is dishonest in very little is also dishonest in much."
>
> Luke 16:10

CHAPTER 6

Lost in Obedience

Lost was generally an obedient daughter. She listened and paid attention to her parents' counsel and advice. Lost's parents encouraged her to be open to them about any concerns related to studies or even affairs of the heart. They advised Lost on which schools to choose and which advanced courses to take. They expected Lost to focus on her studies without relationship distractions.

Because of her obedience, Lost enjoyed the full support of her parents. They trusted Lost and gave her the essential things she needed to succeed in life. In turn, Lost studiously pored over her books and gave her best to make her parents proud. Sure, her parents gave her liberty to take time out and have fun with select friends after school. Lost knew her boundaries and limitations. She didn't want to lose her parents' trust, so she tried to navigate her way out of possible trouble by sticking to her self-imposed curfew, especially during her fun nights out with Merrymaker.

SCENE 7. A STUBBORN STREAK OF INDEPENDENCE

[The surprise party for Confidante was a big success. Several of Confidante's colleagues and friends attended the occasion. One of them was Smooth Talker, a real estate guy. Lost already met Smooth Talker before. Confidante invited him to join in some of their previous days out, hence Lost and Smooth Talker were no strangers to each other. In fact, Lost was kind of impressed with Smooth Talker's charismatic personality and his success in real estate. Also, Smooth Talker's Mom once consulted with Lost about some laboratory test results in connection with a medical issue.]

Smooth Talker: Hello Lost! Wow, you are getting lovelier every time I see you.

Lost: Yeah, yeah, sounds familiar, your standard line whenever we see each other. How's your Mom?

Smooth Talker: She's fine except for some occasional heart palpitations she complains about after a toxic day with Dad.

Lost: Why don't you take your Mom to her cardiologist just to make sure her heart is healthy?

Confidante: Hey, you two, catching up? Smooth Talker, have you asked Lost already?

Lost: About what?

Smooth Talker: Oh Lost, I didn't mean to spring this on you tonight. I'm supposedly waiting for a more appropriate time. Confidante, you and your big mouth.

Lost: Well, I don't mind hearing it now. What is it?

Smooth Talker: I'm organizing a Real Estate Investment Seminar for next Sunday. My goal is to gather as many as one hundred confirmed attendees. The current real estate market is perfect for professionals like you, who wish to earn a huge return with minimum investment in a successful system I'm introducing.

Lost: Really! That sounds very interesting. So how can I help you?

Smooth Talker: Is it possible for you to invite friends in your neighborhood or colleagues at work whom you think will be interested to attend the seminar? I realize it's a big favor and might really be a hassle to you. I would understand if you say no.

Lost: You know what, I don't mind doing you a favor. Let's do it.

[And so, they discussed the details of the planned event. Apparently, Lost wanted to make a good impression on Smooth Talker for reasons her heart only knew. When Lost told her parents about it, her Mom expressed some strong opinions against it.]

Part I: The Story of Good but Lost

Mom Traditionalist: Who is this Smooth Talker? I don't recall you introducing him to your Dad or me. And why are you squandering away your precious time with his real estate business? You're not about to leave home and get your own place without telling us, are you? Look Lost, we know you're an adult now and time is coming when you'll take off and be on your own. We just hope you'll go about it the proper way and we won't be blindsided once it happens.

Lost: Whoa, slow down Mom, you're getting way too melodramatic! Smooth Talker is a good friend. His Mom was once my patient. He's a successful real estate guy and he's very good at what he does. It just so happened that Smooth Talker has an event on Sunday, which I plan to attend. I trust him and I couldn't turn him down.

Mom Traditionalist: Well, I haven't met him yet, which makes it hard for me to trust him. Besides, his event schedule falls on a Sunday. You better not miss church and our Sunday lunch together.

[That Sunday came, and Lost didn't listen to her Mom. She sneaked out early and went with Smooth Talker as she planned.]

> "Children, obey your parents in the Lord, for this is right. 'Honor your father and mother,' which is the first commandment with promise: 'that it may be well with you and you may live long on the earth.'"
>
> Ephesians 6:1–3 (NKJV)

CHAPTER 7

Lost in Passion

When Lost set her mind on something or someone she cared about, she usually turned unapologetically passionate about it. Although Lost was generally mild-mannered and composed, when it came to her desires or pursuits in life, she was unstoppable. Her passion consumed her. Her views and emotions could run high or low depending on the circumstances surrounding the cause, advocacy, thing, or person she was invested in.

SCENE 8. HOOKED ON AN EMOTIONAL RIDE

[A week after the real estate event hosted by Smooth Talker, Lost was still in dreamland. She was hooked on her feelings for Smooth Talker and her newfound interest in real estate. Meanwhile, Lost and her Mom were still not on speaking terms. Mom Traditionalist was giving Lost the silent treatment. Lost on the other hand seemed fine with the situation at home. Real estate became a thing for her because of Smooth Talker. They constantly dated, mixing business and leisure, without the knowledge of Mom Traditionalist.]

Confidante: I see that you and Smooth Talker are getting along great when it comes to real estate. I know that when you're drawn to something, you really pour yourself into it. Imagine, a busy doctor like you finding so much energy for other stuff. I never thought that real estate would interest you.

Part I: The Story of Good but Lost

Lost: I know, right? I too am surprised with myself; I'm learning the ins and outs of buying and selling real estate properties and I find it fascinating. I guess the doctor in me is jumping into the fixer upper properties challenge.

Confidante: Tell me, is it real estate or Smooth Talker that you find fascinating this time?

Lost: Can I say both? Just kidding.

Confidante: What about your Mom? Have you reconciled with her? You should, right?

Lost: I did attempt to make peace, but her ice-cold reception scared me. I'm giving her the space at this time. Don't worry, Mom will come around.

Confidante: It's almost Sunday. You better hurry up so you can all go to church together in peace.

Lost: Oh my God, Sunday! I would have to skip Sunday church again. We made plans to visit this fixer upper property. The client who is my neighbor is only available that time and day. I need to set her up with Smooth Talker for this property inspection. You see, this gets me all excited every time I go with Smooth Talker to see a fixer upper. My creative ideas are really on a free flow, and I don't mind my heart fluttering as well, you know.

Confidante: But Lost, what about your parents and your Wednesday prayer group? Shouldn't you consider at least introducing the guy to your folks? Don't get me wrong, my friend, I know times are different now and I'm happy that you're happy. But it also wouldn't hurt if you do certain things some old fashion way, particularly where family is concerned.

Lost: Oh, come on. I'm sure God will understand, my parents too. Let's face it, as my Mom said, I'm already of age. I know what I'm doing, and right now I really enjoy spending time with Smooth Talker. Who knows where this is even going? Soon they will just let me be with my current fixations. Anyway, if I don't have many patients scheduled for consultation at my clinic, I will surely attend the Wednesday prayer meeting to make up for Sunday.

Confidante: By the way, I have another dear friend in the office who constantly invites me to a bible study at the All for Christ Cornerstone church where she attends. Her name is Mercy Grace.

This time I think I might say yes, just because I'm running out of excuses to tell Mercy Grace. I would love for you to come, so it won't be too awkward for me. Please? It is set next Friday at seven-thirty in the evening.

Lost: Let me see. I don't have clinic that Friday, so sure I will join you then.

> "Keep your heart with all vigilance, for from it flow the springs of life."
>
> Proverbs 4:23

CHAPTER 8

Lost in Sentimentality

The day came when Lost and Confidante attended the bible study at the church where Mercy Grace attends. They felt shy and awkward at first; however, Mercy Grace along with the other friendly church members made them feel welcome as they entered the sanctuary.

SCENE 9. TOUCHED BY GOD'S NEARNESS

[Lost and Confidante were seated in the first row among the hundred young professionals who attended the bible study. A full worship band was set up on stage, and the worship leader began with an opening prayer. Then they started to sing a worship song that speaks of God's unconditional love and grace.]

[Lost and Confidante were wide-eyed throughout worship time. They marveled at the sight of many young people singing together in earnest, the banners containing Scripture verses, and the worship song lyrics flashed on big screens. They found themselves singing heartily along with the congregation. The worship songs started to stir something in them, as they closed their eyes in quiet contemplation at some point. Worship seemed to move them both such that by the final song, they were in tears.]

[Worship ended with the song declaring the Lord Jesus to be the faithful shepherd and overseer of the life and soul of those who choose to put their trust in him.]

Lost in Sentimentality

Lost: My friend, what just happened? Why were we tearing up?

Confidante: I know, as if the songs touched a nerve in me which I don't even understand. I don't recall being moved like this in the church where I go.

Lost: Exactly! I felt like something was broken, feeling sad but at the same time strangely happy. Compared to our neighborhood weekly bible study and prayer meetings, this place is so full of life. Everyone appears to be glad they're here singing to the Lord.

Confidante: What do you do in your meetings, anyway?

Lost: Well, we pray novena prayers, listen to the bible study leader who shares and explains a couple of verses in the bible. The leader then asks anyone who wish to share any stories or experiences related to the verses that we read and studied. Then, we close by reciting the Lord's Prayer together. Before leaving, we eat a sumptuous potluck food feast.

Confidante: That sounds good. How come you say sometimes it feels dry or tedious?

Lost: I admit at times I get weary of the repetitive prayers and storytelling. I find my mind drifting away in the middle of the readings and study. It's kind of different here where worship brims with joy and life. Being here, singing the worship songs, felt as if I'm speaking directly to the Lord, and that he sees and hears me. I've always thought I am with the Lord already, but I've never felt like this before.

Confidante: Well, I felt that way too. I can stand here and continue singing; now I get how delightful it can be to worship Jesus. Let's listen to the bible study teacher coming up.

> "Oh, magnify the Lord with me,
>
> And let us exalt his name together!"
>
> Psalm 34:3

CHAPTER 9

Lost in Rationalism

Still feeling somewhat emotional, the best friends continued to compare notes on what just happened to them during worship. They were at a loss for words to explain what they experienced.

SCENE 10. CONFRONTED WITH THE WORD OF GOD

[Before starting the bible study, Teacher Evangel said this prayer:]

Teacher Evangel: Our heavenly Father, thank you for bringing us all in this sanctuary to praise you and lift the name of Jesus. As we study your Word, may the Holy Spirit give us understanding and insight on how we can apply these truths in our lives. We pray this in the name of Jesus. Amen.

[Then Teacher Evangel asked the congregation to open their bibles in Matthew 19:16-26 (NKJV) and read the passage aloud with him.]

Jesus Counsels the Rich Young Ruler

Now behold, one came and said to Him, "Good Teacher, what good thing shall I do that I may have eternal life?"

So He said to him, "Why do you call Me good? No one is good but One, that is, God. But if you want to enter into life, keep the commandments."

Lost in Rationalism

He said to Him, "Which ones?"

Jesus said, "'You shall not murder,' 'You shall not commit adultery,' 'You shall not steal,' 'You shall not bear false witness,' 'Honor your father and your mother,' and, 'You shall love your neighbor as yourself.'"

The young man said to Him, "All these things I have kept from my youth. What do I still lack?"

Jesus said to him, "If you want to be perfect, go, sell what you have and give to the poor, and you will have treasure in heaven; and come, follow Me."

But when the young man heard that saying, he went away sorrowful, for he had great possessions.

Then Jesus said to His disciples, "Assuredly, I say to you that it is hard for a rich man to enter the kingdom of heaven. And again I say to you, it is easier for a camel to go through the eye of a needle than for a rich man to enter the kingdom of God."

When His disciples heard it, they were greatly astonished, saying, "Who then can be saved?"

But Jesus looked at them and said to them, "With men this is impossible, but with God all things are possible."

[Teacher Evangel proceeded to explain what the bible story meant to the disciples and how it now applies in the present day.]

[Out of everything that was taught and discussed during the bible study, Confidante was deeply provoked with the answer of Jesus to the young man's question, "What do I still lack?" The rich young ruler dutifully knows the commands of God and was obeying them from his youth, and Jesus knew this. The young ruler thought he already met all the conditions that heaven requires to have eternal life because he believed in God and obeyed the commandments. Jesus knew the young man expected an affirmation, but his reply proved the opposite.]

[Lost, on the other hand, deeply empathized with the rich young man. After all, she thought he was a good man who deserved eternal life.]

Part I: The Story of Good but Lost

Confidante: Why would the rich young man address Jesus as "Good Teacher"? And why would he even ask what good thing he must do to have eternal life? He knew the Ten Commandments and he was already keeping them.

Lost: All his life, from his youth, the man considered himself good and carefully followed God's commandments. So I also don't get it why he still thought he lacked some moral qualifications to obtain eternal life. He was already living a perfect life so to speak. Why would he even ask Jesus what he still lacked?

Confidante: I think deep inside, the young man expected Jesus to assure him that he was a good person, supposing that his obedience to God's commandments already qualified him for eternal life. But to his dismay, Jesus challenged the man if he was willing to obey and give up everything to follow him. It turned out he could not give up his wealth, he loved his riches more than he loved God.

[Lost remained quiet for some time, pondering about everything that she heard. Her sympathy went to the rich young man. She was mulling over why the young man needed to sell all his possessions and give to the poor to gain eternal life.]

Lost: That was a sad story. I felt it was unfair for the Lord to ask the young man to sell all his material things and give to the poor. If that were to happen to me, I would reason out with the Lord. I too was brought up in a God-fearing family. Yes, we are well-off, but I'm not flaunting it. In fact, I give generously to people in need. You know me, Confidante. I've been organizing many charity and medical mission projects. I attend weekly bible studies and prayer meetings. I even pray to a few saints. The Lord must be pleased with all these good deeds, right? Aren't these enough? Do I need to be tested and give up everything I have to follow Jesus? If I lose everything, then how will I live? I cannot be dependent on my parents forever. How would I be able to serve and do charity if I lose all my savings and possessions?

Confidante: Well, this is also making me question my own standing, hearing the story of this rich young man. Am I still failing God in some areas of my life that I'm not aware of? That young man had preconceived ideas on what makes a person good, and probably reasonably believes that heaven rewards good deeds with eternal life. Remember his words when he addressed Jesus as "Good Teacher"? To this however, Jesus replied, "Why do you call me good? No one is good except God alone."

Could it be that our notion of goodness is different from God's? The things that we consider to be good for our souls, are these the same things that God finds good and acceptable? If not, then what do we need to do to enter heaven? What does Jesus mean when he said that there is no one good except God?

Above all I think the most pressing question for us is—how will we respond if Jesus asked us today to drop everything that we treasure in life and go follow him?

> "For what does it profit a man to gain the whole world and forfeit his soul? For what can a man give in return for his soul?"
>
> Mark 8:36–37

CHAPTER 10

Lost in Contrast with Confidante

After the bible study, Lost carried on with her life routine as usual. The emotional high she felt at the church service quickly subsided. On the other hand, Confidante continued to seek and ask the Lord. The words of Jesus in Scripture and the response of the rich young man weighed heavily in Confidante's mind. It made her curious and restless as she thought about her own spiritual condition. She read the bible passage again and again and thought hard about it. Deep within, she didn't want to be like the rich young man. She didn't want to say "no" to Jesus if ever.

SCENE 11. A CONVERSATION WITH GOD

Confidante: Lord, is there anything in my life that is not right in your eyes? I keep the commandments. I don't have known enemies. I attend church regularly. I'm living a decent life. But why do I feel this way, as if I'm unsettled by something I can't fully explain? Search my heart, O God. If my good deeds do not lead me to you, please show me the way. During worship time Lord, I felt a different kind of joy, like you were present, hearing us and receiving our songs. Being with those young Christians who love you felt so heavenly. But beyond those feelings, the study of your word disturbed my mind. Help me know who you really are Lord Jesus, not just learn facts about you.

[Confidante eventually fell asleep with her thoughts set on the Lord.]

> "Let us know; let us press on to know the Lord;
> his going out is sure as the dawn;
> he will come to us as the showers,
> as the spring rains that water the earth."
>
> Hosea 6:3

SCENE 12. PERSONAL FRIENDSHIP WITH JESUS

[The morning after, Confidante got a call from her co-worker, Mercy Grace.]

Confidante: Hello, Mercy Grace. I'm so happy you called.

Mercy Grace: Oh Confidante, I'm happier because you finally joined us last night at the bible study. So how are you? Would you like to come again to next week's study?

Confidante: You bet. I will be there next week. I'm taking the opportunity to learn more about the Lord through the study of his Word. I do have some questions to ask you though.

Mercy Grace: What a joy to hear this! Indeed, Jesus promises to reveal himself to those who honestly seek him. This is one decision that you will not regret. How about we meet up today at lunch or after work if you prefer?

Confidante: Sure, lunchtime would be great. See you then.

[Lunchtime in the office cafeteria, Mercy Grace and Confidante were visibly both excited chatting about that eventful night.]

Confidante: I can't thank you enough for inviting me to your bible study. The worship, the teaching on the story of the rich young man, the fellowship with your church friends, all gave me a sense of God's presence which felt so real. I'm beginning to understand now why you keep telling us about how good the Lord is, and why I always see you reading scripture. And yes, your prayers sound so personal and sincere. Tell me, were you always like this?

Mercy Grace: No. I used to be a very introverted person. I never really had constant friends since I seldom attended social gatherings. I felt more comfortable just doing stuff on my own. I loved to read self-help books. I lost my Mom when I was thirteen. My Dad was not always around either. He put me through school and provided for my education, and that was it. So pretty much, I was self-driven, independent, overcoming life's challenges on my own. I am neither a religious person nor a heretic. I believe there is a God, but I thought he was just up there, looking on us below. God felt distant during that time.

Confidante: So, what changed?

Mercy Grace: I was graduating from college that year. I was having a tough time at home and in school, emotionally and mentally. I had no study group. I was stressed out with school, with my Dad, and with my relationship. There were a couple of subjects that I was struggling with. I almost dropped out from those classes because I thought I would fail, and I couldn't afford a repeat. There was a ton of schoolwork to pass before the final exams. I had a major disagreement with my Dad, and my boyfriend was ghosting me. All the distress piled up at the same time! I had no one to talk to and it was just too much to handle. Normally I would rely on myself and say *I can do this*, but that time was different. I was in a desperate place, exhausted, and honestly lost. I remember thinking, if God was out there, let me try him. And so I said, *God, this time I cannot do it. Help me. I don't know what to do.*

Not long after, my phone rang. It was Miss Thoughtful, my former learning mentor in secondary school. Back then, she helped a lot of students, including me, overcome problems concerning our studies. In our failures, she always encouraged us to press on. She was one of the kindest, most encouraging people I know. Every time we parted ways, she always assured me that she was praying for me and all the other struggling students.

She called to invite me to an Alumni Homecoming event that she was organizing, not knowing what I was going through that day. I thanked Miss Thoughtful for the call but could hardly contain my sobbing; the hopelessness and pressure were eating me up. Miss Thoughtful sensed the predicament I was in. She began assuring me that I need not go through all my troubles alone. The love of Jesus is always available, and if I ask him to help carry my burdens, he would. She reminded me of these words from Scripture:

> "Come to Me, all you who labor and are heavy laden, and I will give you rest."
>
> Matthew 11:28 (NKJV)

> "Do not be anxious about anything, but in everything by prayer and supplication with thanksgiving let your requests be made known to God. And the peace of God, which surpasses all understanding, will guard your hearts and your minds in Christ Jesus."
>
> Philippians 4:6–7

Hearing the word of God at that moment was like a fresh breeze; it kind of cleared the fog that gripped my head. It dawned on me that although I don't have all the answers to everything, the Lord certainly does. I asked Miss Thoughtful to pray for me and she did. That night, I resolved to submit and depend on Jesus, I asked him to help me deal with my troubles.

To be clear, I still needed to work on passing my course exams and to settle my issues with Dad and my boyfriend, but the surety that my Lord would help me sort through it was real. I really believed that as I ran to God for help, he would not turn his back on me. From then on, I prayed every day for God to help me.

Miss Thoughtful pointed me to a Christian church where I attended discipleship studies in the ways of Christ. I applied myself diligently to reading and examining the truths in God's word. Slowly I began to understand the reality of my sins, that by nature my heart was inclined to love myself and the world more than God. In my self-sufficient ways, I did not realize how far away I was from the Lord. I began to see my own shortcomings—in attitude, words, and behavior—toward God and toward the people around me. I needed God to forgive me.

I struggled to persevere in prayer, to be grateful particularly at times when it appeared there was nothing to be thankful for. It was hard especially in the beginning; it was so tempting to just spend time streaming movies or catching up with friends on social media, rather than pray. But I didn't want to miss out on becoming friends with Jesus. I didn't want to miss what he wanted to teach me in his Word. As I pressed on, by God's grace I started understanding who Jesus really is—what he has done for us, and the life and joy he intends to give us. It turns out that when you come to know the Lord more and more, you become mindful to put him first even in everyday decisions. When you begin to really understand what Jesus did and went through because of how much he loves you, it is hard to stay unchanged; it becomes difficult not to love him back.

Again, mind you, this was not as easy as it sounds. If we take certain things in this world seriously like school and career, why not apply the same diligence about our soul? What could be more important than faith and the safety of our soul? These thoughts moved me to press on and get a clear understanding of what saving faith really means.

So grateful to God for providing the means for instruction and grace to take root in my life—like spending time in Scripture, personal prayers, worship, getting connected at my church, and the encouragement of like-minded Christian friends. These helped me a lot in my faith walk. I learned to manage things one day at a time, and mindfully did things best that I could, in line with what I read in the bible. Until slowly I began noticing my own desires, attitude, and perspective on things changed. And day after day after day, my relationships with people around me became lighter and more joyful.

[Confidante listened intently to the testimonial story of Mercy Grace as it made a significant impression on her.]

> "The Lord is my strength and my shield;
> My heart trusted in Him, and I am helped;
> Therefore my heart greatly rejoices,
> And with my song I will praise Him."
>
> Psalm 28:7 (NKJV)

CHAPTER 11

Lost in Compromises

Meanwhile, Lost and her Mom remained cold and distant toward each other, this even after Lost attended the bible study at Mercy Grace's church a few days back. Lost got right back to her normal daily routine. She continued living her life the best way she knew how, relying on herself and doing well to others.

Lost believed in the humanist and New Age philosophies. She agreed with the mantra mentioned in a TV talk show—*Only what you can do for Christ will last*. The mantra says that if you replace the word "Christ" with "goodness" or "grace," then whatever you do in this world would last. If you can change somebody's life, then yours gets changed in return. What counts is using what you have, no matter what station of life you are in, to give to others, benefitting both giver and recipient. At the outset, this idea sounds harmless, even noble. The idea behind it was based on a bible verse in the book of Corinthians (2 Corinthians 5:9–10). But in truth, the Scripture verse was quoted out of context, and has totally distorted the original verse's intent. Christ is taken out of the equation, and the good things that the self does become front and center. Christ is stripped away, dislodged from the place of honor, and the do-gooder self is exalted.

Part I: The Story of Good but Lost

SCENE 13. THE TEMPTATION OF FREE STUFF

Patient Freelance: Doc, I don't have health insurance. I cannot afford expensive diagnostic tests. I do freelance work and right now I'm in between projects. I don't have a regular monthly income.

Lost: Don't worry, I'm waiving my professional fee. I will refer you to my resident doctor who's doing a diagnostic test research study using a new machine. He has enough volunteers already for the trial procedure but I will talk him into bumping off one patient to make room for you. That way you won't have to pay anything.

Patient Freelance: Doc, thank you for your kindness. Please do refer me as a volunteer.

Lost: I will just prescribe a couple of meds for you today. My assistant will keep you posted on the test procedure.

[Another patient, who is a friend of Lost, entered the clinic for a personal request. She wasn't sick of anything.]

Patient Fibber: Doc, may I request for a medical certificate? I took a couple of sick days driving around and taking care of some personal matters. I might get in trouble if I don't present a certificate when I report back to work. It is hectic at work these days, but I just thought I should use my sick days even though I'm not sick, to get some errands and personal transactions done.

Lost: Sure, I will write one for you, my friend. I don't want you to have trouble going back to work, just in case.

Patient Fibber: Thank you so much, Doc. You're really the best.

[After Lost's friend left, a familiar medical representative cut in line to talk to the doctor.]

Assistant Efficient: Doc, it's your trusted medical representative, Mr. Bribe.

Mr. Bribe: Hi Doc! We're introducing a new drug in the market. It has been tested safe and highly recommended for its efficacy. I'm leaving you lots of samples.

Lost: Great! I'll make sure to review the literature and see if some of my patients can benefit from this new drug therapy.

Mr. Bribe: By the way, I've already booked your flight and hotel accommodations for the World Congress on Health Informatics in a beautiful island in the south, all expenses paid. It's on the weekend after next, Saturday to Monday.

Lost: Can I bring my best friend with me? Even if she's not attending the conference, can you cover her flight and accommodations?

Mr. Bribe: Sure, we can arrange to accommodate her as your family. Thanks for keeping our pharmaceutical company in your prescription drug list for your patients. See you at the conference, Doc.

Lost: Sure, see you then.

> "Do not be conformed to this world, but be transformed by the renewal of your mind, that by testing you may discern what is the will of God, what is good and acceptable and perfect."
>
> Romans 12:2

CHAPTER 12

Lost in Devotion

With sheer excitement, Lost couldn't wait to blurt out her good news to her friend. She was pretty sure Confidante would be overjoyed.

SCENE 14. A SURPRISE REJECTION

Lost: Hi Confidante. I have a surprise treat for you, a trip to your dream destination—the Mountain View Island!

Confidante: Wow, really? I've always wanted to visit that gorgeous island but just couldn't find the opportunity.

Lost: Don't worry about it. I asked a favor from my favorite medical representative. We have this physician's conference sponsored by a pharmaceutical company. I told the medical rep that I will bring my best friend with me as family member. No questions asked, he readily said yes. All expenses paid for you.

Confidante: What? How is that possible? My flight and hotel accommodations would be shouldered by the pharmaceutical company? But I have nothing to do with that conference.

Lost: Oh dear. This is in your bucket list, so I had to take you with me.

Confidante: Is that even allowed? I'm not your family, just a friend. I kind of feel guilty about this. I feel it's not right, dishonest for me to take advantage of your sponsored trip.

Lost in Devotion

Lost: Come on, Confidante, everybody is doing this. Nowadays, it's sort of an accepted practice not just in the medical field but in other trade conferences as well. Can't you just be excited over this freebie trip? It's scheduled on the weekend after next, Saturday to Monday. It's going to be fun for sure.

Confidante: On a weekend? I'm sorry, Lost. Now I have no choice but to decline. I don't feel right about it, and I also can't miss church and work. The bible study with Mercy Grace spoke strongly to me; it got me thinking about my relationship with the Lord. I didn't see it coming, but I'm beginning to re-assess my priorities now. I appreciate your generosity but first things first. And how about you and your Mom? She will be hurt again, not seeing you at church on Sunday.

Lost: Stop preaching, Confidante! I'm really very disappointed and offended. I thought this will make you happy, but here you are lecturing me with moral issues where there is none. If you don't want to go, fine!

Confidante: Oh, my dear Lost, I'm very sorry. I didn't mean to offend you in any way. I hope you'd understand where I'm coming from. Please don't let this trip come between us. We've been the best of friends for the longest time.

> "So whoever knows the right thing to do and fails to do it, for him it is sin."
>
> James 4:17

CHAPTER 13

Lost in Offenses

Lost considered herself to be an upright person, but she was often critical of people who did not measure up to her standards of goodness and excellence. This was ironic as she easily took offense at criticisms and rejection. When Lost was angry, pride always got in the way, and it usually took her long to come around. It was hard for her to apologize, especially if she believed she was in the right. Lost was the type of person who could live with having estranged relationships for years.

Confidante, on the other hand, diligently attended the bible study classes and immersed herself in daily reading of God's word. She had come to regard Scripture as a means of instruction, a trustworthy guide to inquire of the Lord especially when she has pressing questions and decisions to make.

Confidante was not compelled by any outside person or religion, but by the conviction that she could develop a friendship with the living God. She finally understood that being good is more than engaging in pious works or having a decent life. True faith prompts a lifestyle of continuously choosing God over things of the world. Although not easy, Confidante started to practice upholding biblical values in her everyday routine. Many times, she faltered and fell short, but she asked God to forgive her and help her become better. This remarkable change in character was beginning to take hold in Confidante amidst her conflict with Lost.

Lost, in contrast, only experienced an emotional high and temporary godliness that day she attended the bible study with Confidante. The next day, those emotions faded away as Lost returned to her usual self-reliant ways.

Overcoming her hurt, Lost prayed her novena and asked God to enlighten Confidante. In the following days, Lost continued to ignore Confidante's calls. She decided to meet up with Smooth Talker to vent her frustrations with Confidante.

SCENE 15. THE FRIENDLY BIAS ADVICE

Lost: I just need someone who will listen, someone who will understand. I thought of you, since we're both friends with Confidante. I appreciate you came.

Smooth Talker: Of course, I'm here for you. What is it that's bothering you?

Lost: You know that I care about Confidante, right? We've been friends way back in high school. We practically grew up together; she's like the sister I never had. I've always been generous to her because she deserves it. However, a few days ago, Confidante hurt me big time.

Smooth Talker: I've always known Confidante to be super cool. She has constantly looked up to you and considered you as her friend with a big heart. What happened?

Lost: Well, I've arranged for her to join me in a surprise treat to this beautiful island, which I know is in her bucket list of places to see. It's all expenses paid by the business company sponsoring the medical conference that I'm attending. Instead of being happy and grateful, she turned it down and gave me an earful about how morally wrong it is for her to accept this free trip.

Smooth Talker: What? Confidante did that? That was unfair. What is wrong about taking the company-sponsored offer and joining you in this trip? I totally get how awful you must feel. You didn't deserve that kind of rejection and rebuke. Your generosity to your friend is perhaps too much?

Part I: The Story of Good but Lost

Lost: She is my good friend that's why I'm so hurt. I've been ignoring her calls and haven't talked to her since. She sent me text messages explaining her convictions and take on the issue. She even had my favorite food delivered to my house as peace offering. However, I still can't get over how she responded. I need time to heal.

Smooth Talker: Sure, you need that space to recover. How can I help? Would you like to come with me to the open house I'm staging this weekend? You know, to relax and take your mind off things.

Lost: Oh, Smooth Talker, you're such a good listener. Thank you for understanding my situation. Yes, I would love to go out with you, but maybe to a movie and dinner afterwards. Tonight?

[The two hugged affectionately and left for a spur of the moment date night to forget about Confidante.]

> "Better is open rebuke than hidden love.
> Faithful are the wounds of a friend;
> profuse are the kisses of an enemy."

Proverbs 27:5–6

CHAPTER 14

Lost in Brokenness

Confidante repeatedly reached out to Lost, in hopes to settle and resolve their difference. Lost however decided to ignore Confidante and kept distant.

Confidante pressed on with her newfound joy of walking with Christ, immersing herself in bible reading, and fellowship with her new friends at church. She marveled at how the bible study teachings gradually gave her clarity in understanding who God is and what he has done through Jesus. As Confidante grew in the knowledge of God, she began to recognize her many wrong presumptions about her own goodness. She wrestled with the truths on what the bible says about her sinful nature, about how God the Father sees her without Jesus in her life.

The day of reckoning came when Confidante finally knew what was lacking in her perceived good life. God made her realize that she was still a sinner like the rest of the unbelieving world. The Lord has faithfully dealt with her many questions, including the queries she had with the story of the rich young ruler, and why it said that no one is good except God alone. She finally came to understand that the goodness that pleases God comes from within a changed heart, not from any external deed. This brought Confidante to a place of repentance and faith. She realized that she needed to ask forgiveness for how she led her life according to her own standards of goodness, and not according to the righteousness acceptable to God through faith in Jesus.

SCENE 16. THE SURRENDERED LIFE AND THE WAYWARD LIFE

Confidante: After spending a long time carefully examining the word of God and seeking the Lord in prayer, I've come to realize that it's time for me to stop going about things my own way. True life can only be found in the opposite direction—by setting aside my own will and asking God in faith for his will and purpose in my life. Would you lead me in prayer?

Mercy Grace: Oh yes, I'm so grateful to God for drawing you to make this life-changing decision. The angels in heaven must surely be rejoicing over you as you yield your life to Christ. Come let's pray this prayer of repenting from your sins and receiving Jesus as your Lord.

[On the other hand, Lost seemed to be teetering on the edge. She got extremely stressed out with her work at the hospital and began faltering here and there. Her mood swings made the people around her uptight. For the first time ever, two of her patients died under her watch. One day, after seeing her last patient in the clinic, Lost wept by herself and started calling out to God.]

Lost: Oh God, what is happening to me? Why do I feel so miserable? I've been living a perfect life so far, what went wrong? Why do I feel so burdened now, first my Mom, then Confidante, now these troubles and failures in my practice. All my life I've been a good daughter, responsible with my studies and work, a loyal friend. I go out of my way to help people. I've worked hard to build a reputable medical practice. I don't deserve all this disappointing mess. It feels so unfair.

Lost's Inner Conscience: Maybe because you have been missing church with your family lately. You have not reconciled with your Mom. After many weeks, you haven't said a single word to her.

Lost: All my life, I've been attending church and prayer meetings with my family. I've been an obedient daughter. I've only been skipping church lately due to my busier schedule and some disagreements with my Mom. God, are you punishing me for this?

Lost's Inner Conscience: You might have reneged in some other ways, like your charity works. You have been too busy lately with your personal concerns that you have not responded to any requests for help.

Lost: Does it make me a bad person if I'm not able to help or assist other people groups lately? Was that so wrong of me, God?

[Weary and discouraged, Lost did not go home on purpose and instead checked in at a staycation hotel by herself. She sobbed as she poured out all her frustrations and bitterness over the troubles that were happening in her life. She cried herself to sleep.]

[The morning after, Lost woke up and oddly found herself humming a familiar tune in her head. It was one of the songs they sang at the bible study she attended with Confidante. The song lyrics in her mind somehow calmed her down and left her uttering, "Thank you, God."]

[Her cell phone rang. It was her Mom who sounded so concerned about Lost not coming home last night. The mother and daughter found themselves on speaking terms again after many weeks of cold silence. This helped eased the downcast spirit of Lost. She collected herself and was again ready to face a new day; although there still lingered a sense of emptiness in her that she couldn't shake off. Lost promised her Mom she would be home for dinner after her work in the hospital.]

> "Therefore let anyone who thinks that he stands take heed lest he fall."
>
> 1 Corinthians 10:12

CHAPTER 15

Lost is Lost

It was the weekend to travel outside the city for the medical conference. Lost packed her bags and headed to the airport by herself. At the airport, while waiting to board the plane, Lost thought it would have been more fun if Confidante came. She wanted to call her friend, but her heart wasn't ready to forgive yet.

Meanwhile, at that exact time, Confidante was doing her daily quiet time with God.

SCENE 17. THE PRAYER AND MISSION

Confidante: Father God, please bless and protect us all, church workers and volunteers, in this mission trip for the homeless and depressed communities in the south. Anoint us with your love as we provide some help for their physical needs and share the gospel. Grant them understanding, Almighty God, so that they may come to know and trust in Jesus.

And Lord, I also remember in prayer my dear friend Lost. Please heal her emotions and move her to forgive me. Please draw her in saving faith to Jesus. Fill her mind with the peace that only you can give. Thank you, Lord, for you love Lost more than she can ever know. Keep Lost in your providential care. Amen.

[After her personal prayers, Confidante proceeded to the airport to join her church mission team for their flight to the south that weekend.]

> "Continue steadfastly in prayer, being watchful in it with thanksgiving."
>
> Colossians 4:2

SCENE 18. THE ILL-FATED FLIGHT

[Lost was waiting to board the plane. She was oblivious of the other physicians who were with her on this trip. Lost was glad to get away for a change of environment, but she was not really thrilled. Her thoughts were still unsettled, concerning the patients that she lost and the misunderstanding with Confidante. When boarding time was announced, she was tempted to give Confidante a call as she thought to herself . . .]

Lost: Should I call Confidante? But I am the one who is hurt. Why should I be the first to call? Should I just swallow my pride and call her? What if she doesn't answer? What if she ignores my call? What if she says something hurtful again?

[Lost reluctantly called Confidante. As the phone rang, before Confidante could pick up, Lost hung up. Her pride decided against it.]

Flight Attendant: Final call for boarding, calling all passengers of South Air Pacific, Flight SAP 101 bound to Mountain View Island. This is your last call for boarding, proceed to Gate Four.

[Lost and her colleagues all boarded the plane and off they flew.]

[After over three hours of turbulent flight, the plane finally prepared for descent. As the plane was coming down, it began to shake wildly and uncontrollably. The pilot tried to maneuver the landing, but it was too late; the plane crash landed before it could reach the airport runway.]

Lost: Oh my God, oh my God . . . [Screaming, loud cries, and piercing explosions filled the air.]

Part I: The Story of Good but Lost

"And do you seek great things for yourself? Seek them not, for behold, I am bringing disaster upon all flesh, declares the Lord . . . ."

Jeremiah 45:5

PART II

The Measure of Good People—
Worldly Perspective

CHAPTER 16

The Characteristics of Good People

Whether we acknowledge it or not, the story of Lost strikes a familiar chord in almost everyone. Either at one time we lived like Lost, or we know someone who lives like Lost and may not even know it. This someone may be in our family, school, workplace, neighborhood, or church. Many of them are well-meaning, likable, engaging individuals who have been taught and raised well by wonderful parents/grandparents. Many are well-educated, work hard on their business or craft, church goers, and are all-around contributing members of their communities.

Like Lost, they tick off all the check boxes in the nice, good people list. A quick survey of the standout characteristics of the good people group as perceived by the world may look something like these:

- *Generous*—these good people are the antithesis of Mr. Scrooge (before he became a changed man). They love to give gifts and they cheerfully foot the bill when dining out, especially when in the company of trusted friends. Generous giving though is not necessarily the same as sacrificial giving; most generous givers are predisposed to give out of the surplus of their pockets. Generous people are likely to share not just money or material things, but also their time, opinions, and expertise. Not only can they be counted on to sign up and volunteer for worthy causes, but their enthusiastic involvement usually helps attract more people to join the charity projects. The world looks up to this energetic group of people who gives above and beyond the ordinary.

- *Religious*—these good people acknowledge that there must be a greater spiritual entity ordering the affairs of man, whether it be God or another higher being. Friends and family often ask them for wise counsel or prayers, because they either follow a spiritual sage/guru or they pray to special saints whom they believe facilitate intercessions to God. Church is typically the first order of the day on Sundays for most in this group. Many sing in the church choir, teach in Sunday school, or participate in lay ministry service. They mark holy calendar feasts or open their homes for prayer activities. Some have even installed icons in their homes to pray to.

- *Self-Driven*—these good people possess the drive to achieve and make something out of themselves. They thrive in areas of intellectual pursuits, competitive sports, managing a business, even planting churches, or expanding church ministries. The world looks up to these individuals who fix their eyes on lofty goals and devote their lives to achieving them. Motivational mantras like "Action Conquers Fear" or "Yes You Can, Yes You Will" underscore the energy and passion of many in this group. The world celebrates and cheers them who push hard and set themselves apart in the name of excellence, service, or making a difference.

- *Independent*—these good people are the self-sufficient ones. Using their own wisdom and abilities, they do all they can to find the means to fend for themselves and their families. The world loves them because they think ahead and methodically prepare their go-to plans and backup plans, execute those plans, and so secure their future. On the way up, they follow the written rules, work hard, master the nuts and bolts of their craft, and refrain from bothering others if they can help it. These people hardly ask for favors. They work extra hard so as not to burden anyone. They are self-made and secure in themselves. They do not lack for anything.

The Characteristics of Good People

Our world is full of such nice, exemplary people who conform to all manners and ways deemed praiseworthy and good by the world. On the surface, there is nothing wrong with the cares and aspirations that preoccupy our do-gooder list. Many of us were brought up and encouraged to do the same—to always give our best, do good, and be good. And indeed, we should.

The question we venture to ask concerning our pursuit of excellence and good works is, where does God stand in all of it? Wouldn't it be interesting to know what God says or thinks about our acts of service?

How is it that many who live successful lives and do good works may actually be on the same path as Lost? If there is goodness that leads to eternal life, as the title of this book suggests, could there also be goodness that keeps man away from heaven?

What makes good works acceptable or unacceptable in the sight of God?

CHAPTER 17

The Heart of Good Works

People who honestly believe that they walk in goodness, without abiding in Christ, are treading on a dead-end road, full of pitfalls. The goodness that is approved of God is one that comes from a gospel-changed heart, as differentiated from outward forms of goodness. The good works over which the Lord delights emanate or flow from a heart and will that seek to honor and obey him. As Jesus says in the book of John:

> "I am the vine; you are the branches. Whoever abides in me and I in him, he it is that bears much fruit, for apart from me you can do nothing."
>
> John 15:5

Our kindness, generosity, and diligence in practicing our moral duties will remain fruitless unless our lives are intentionally attuned to Christ. The image depicted for us in the above verse is that we are the branches attached to the vine who is Christ. The vine gives life and nourishment to the branches, without which, no fruit can be produced. As branches, we are dependent on the vine; we need to remain connected to Jesus if we are to bear fruit. Apart from him, our striving to do well towards others and build successful lives for ourselves may make us feel in bliss for a season, but this hardly endures. Outward obedience alone, without prayerful examination of the heart towards Christ, is skin deep and does not disturb the conscience.

To help us understand how this looks, let's revisit the story of our character Lost.

At the outset, everything was going great for her. Lost was an outstanding student, dutiful daughter, high achiever, with a thriving medical practice, respected by her peers. She had enduring relationships and friendships. And she devoted time and resources to all sorts of charities left and right.

Her lifeboat was sailing along smoothly and steadily until the waters underneath started to swell, and we see the inner character of Lost slowly unravel. Confronted with various circumstances, we witness how Lost acted and reacted with moral turpitude, insensitive words, a puffed-up sense of self, and an unforgiving spirit. She gossiped about the failures of others and sustained a grudge with her Mom over a disagreement. We see her in total conformity with what the world sees as frivolous and honest mistakes, as the case with her undercharged credit cards.

We also see Lost's lack of conviction over pulling strings, trading favors with associates in the pharmaceutical company, and issuing bogus medical certificates as favors for friends. Her heightened sense of self made it tough for her to consider and accept contrary views or ideas from others. Her quickness to judge people over one overlooked task, tendency to take deep offense over those who decline her generosity, propensity to hold grudges, and refusal to forgive—all these exhibit a mind and heart that are contrary to Christ. The world may see no real harm in these things, but they clearly point to a character that is not walking and abiding in Christ.

Lost's life took an unexpected turn in a sudden tragedy, the ending of which was not revealed in the story. If her life ended that day, surely many would say that Lost had gone up to heaven. Why so? Because the world perceives Lost to be a good person—someone who excelled in her pursuits, gave generously to others, and never burdened anyone.

But didn't God create us for a life of good works? Indeed, the bible contains many teachings that call for men to be kind to others, generous to those in need, hospitable to strangers, and

Part II: The Measure of Good People—Worldly Perspective

compassionate to the sick. Many believe that if we do not grow weary in doing good, God must surely bless us and reward us with eternal life. Our main character Lost exhibited many desirable traits and lived an outstanding life. In her own self-assessment, Lost knew that she helped a lot of people and did admirable things, hence God must be pleased with her. But when things took a downward turn and she started experiencing setbacks in life, Lost's inflated ego and self-worth couldn't take it and had her questioning God. *What did I miss? I don't deserve this. I did everything right, why is all this happening to me?* Lost saw herself the way the world normally sees and affirms her kind—someone who is worthy to be blessed by the heavens because they work hard and make every effort to live in moral standing before God and men.

Until our eyes are opened to see our own inadequacies and learn that our life is not ultimately ordered by us, it is very difficult for us to stop trusting in ourselves. This is particularly true among the many decent, responsible, successful people who work hard to secure their worth. Once trouble hits, we exhaust everything within our human ability to fix the problem. Many of us run to God for help only when we come to the end of ourselves.

But what does God think about these things? What does God's word say about people whose faith rests on their presumed goodness? How does God look at Lost and the life she lived? What about you? If a sudden event brings you face to face with God, what do you suppose God will say about the life you lived?

As one of the authors of this book (D. Alonzo) confesses, "I too was just like Lost in more ways than one. I used to think I was approved of God because I was a church goer, good daughter, honor student, and cheerful friend. In self-retrospect, I realized on the flipside, I was also proud, selfish, impatient, and opinionated."

"I was not fully aware of my own shortcomings and weaknesses since the evil one blinded me into believing that I was living a good life as a nice and smart young girl. I had a religion that I thought connected me with God but did not really give me a clear understanding of who God truly is and what God did for me. Only when confronted with the truth of God's word did I realize that I was a sinner needing a Savior. For all my religiosity, I was in fact

The Heart of Good Works

lost. The word of God made me realize that the righteousness I thought I had was like filthy rags in the eyes of God. It is of utmost importance to make sure that our view of religion and saving faith is clear and grounded in the truths of God."

Outward appearances can be deceiving. No matter how good we are on the outside, we all wrestle with temptations and experience moral failings in life. That is why we cannot really say if somebody is good or bad, saved or unsaved, based on externals alone. Man cannot see one's inner heart and motivation, only God can.

There is only one trustworthy way to understand ourselves—and that is by knowing who God is and what God has done for us. Understanding ourselves based on what other people say we are or based on what we do for others is unwise, as it is likely to give us a flawed or deceptive picture. In our quest to understand goodness, the same principle applies. We can only begin to comprehend what true goodness is once we have a biblical understanding of who God is and what he has done for man.

Author Phil Ryken, in his book *Loving Jesus More*, said this about the story of the rich young ruler in the bible:

> "Jesus did not expose the rich young ruler's pretensions to holiness by disputing his claim to sinless perfection, but instead by giving him one simple test on whether God was first in the man's life or not. Jesus told the rich young ruler to sell everything and give away all the proceeds. In making this demand, he was not saying that we can win our way to heaven simply by giving away all our wealth. No, the requirement for salvation is faith in Jesus Christ. But in this particular case, Jesus identified the one area of the ruler's life where he refused to love God above all."[1]

Considering the truths we've discussed so far, it behooves us to ask these difficult questions and attempt to find honest answers to them:

In all our perseverance to live an upright life, how much of it is grounded in the measure used by God? Can we really work our

---

1. Ryken, *Loving Jesus More*, 105–106.

way to becoming good without heeding the truths and warnings laid down for us in God's word?

Since the bible says it is appointed for man once to die and then comes judgment (Hebrews 9:27), when such time comes and God takes account of our earthly lives, will he find the good life that we lived sufficient or wanting?

Is it possible for us to be good yet be lost forever?

If we believe in the eternality of our soul and care about it, we must beware in supposing or assuming that our sterling family background, spotless reputation, religion, moral advocacies, and pious works will secure us a place in heaven. A self-assured heart that rests upon the standards of goodness promoted by the world can be a perilous thing.

If this is the case, it befits us to ask, what sort of goodness then will assure us a place in heaven?

> "But the Lord said to Samuel, 'Do not look on his appearance or on the height of his stature, because I have rejected him. For the Lord sees not as man sees: man looks on the outward appearance, but the Lord looks on the heart.'"
>
> 1 Samuel 16:7

PART III

The Attributes of a Good God—Biblical Perspective

CHAPTER 18

What God Says is Good

To be clear, it is not any man's business including ours to say which or what action counts as good. The heart of this book is not to dictate who is good and who is not. This prerogative belongs to God alone because only he can read the heart and mind of man.

This book, however, advocates the view that it is well for man to learn and consider the sort of goodness that lines up with the word of God. It is to our benefit to know and understand what God says is good, and guard against what the world promotes as good. The value of doing so can be life changing. King David affirmed this admonition for us in Psalm 119:72–73, "The law of your mouth is better to me than thousands of gold and silver pieces. Your hands have made and fashioned me; give me understanding that I may learn your commandments."

By now, you would have been familiar with the parable concerning the rich young ruler, since we have repeatedly referenced it in the previous chapters. In it, the young man asked Jesus a question and addressed him as good teacher. To this, Jesus called the young man out, "Why do you call me good? No one is good except God alone" (Luke 18:19).

In our quest to understand who and what is good, it is a helpful place to start with Jesus' unmistakable words. The Lord himself clearly declares that God alone is good. Therefore, anybody else who claims to be good is a liar. We take Jesus at his word because he knows the Father fully (John 10:30; John 13:3). While rightfully affirming that God the Father is good, Jesus though is not negating that he is good. The rich young man's idea of goodness—borne out of a humanistic worldview—needed to be addressed. Jesus is redirecting the eyes of the young man to God as the source of everything good.

So, do you think the goodness of people like the rich ruler or even our story's character Lost would qualify for eternal life? Like them, many believers claim to follow the basic moral laws taught under the Ten Commandments.

Take for instance the commandment, "You shall not murder." Many of us who live decent, productive lives consider this command one of the easier ones to follow. We say it is far removed from our nature to physically hurt another, let alone take another's life. Having said this, it comes as a surprise to many that in the court of God, you can be found guilty of murder even without physically taking someone else's life. Jesus explains in Matthew 5:21–22, "You have heard that it was said to those of old, 'You shall not murder; and whoever murders will be liable to judgment.' But I say to you that everyone who is angry with his brother will be liable to judgment; whoever insults his brother will be liable to the council; and whoever says, 'You fool!' will be liable to the hell of fire."

In other words, Scripture says that the sin of murder begins not with the hands, but with our thoughts and heart. Think of how many people we have wounded and how many relationships we have burned with our careless and hurtful words. "Death and life are in the power of the tongue," says Proverbs 18:21. Our vicious and reckless words can kill, destroy, or ruin a person. In the eyes of God, having an angry and unforgiving attitude toward another, customarily expressed in our words, may be tantamount to murder.

The same goes for the command, "You shall not commit adultery." Scores of loving and faithful husbands and wives all over the world profess that not once did they ever commit adultery. This is because they never broke their vow of conjugal chastity and physical exclusivity with their marital spouse. But hear what Jesus says about this in Matthew 5:27–28, "You have heard that it was said, 'You shall not commit adultery.' But I say to you that everyone who looks at a woman with lustful intent has already committed adultery with her in his heart." In the precepts of God, adultery once conceived in the heart can be consummated in the sinful eyes of man.

All this is to illustrate that God observes the thoughts, intents, and preoccupations of man. The posture of the heart, from which words and actions emanate, matters foremost to God. While man can play nice and be seen as praiseworthy by the world, he can never hide from and deceive God. The Lord knows whose are his, "My sheep hear my voice, and I know them, and they follow me" (John 10:27).

CHAPTER 19

Good Works that Lead to God

To be clear, this book must not be construed as negating, trashing, or diminishing the good works done by men. We are not saying that God rejects good works in and of itself—there are many sincere people who do works of mercy out of fear of God, humility, kindness, and genuine concern for others. They believe in God but may not know Jesus Christ yet as Savior and Lord.

As believers, we are cognizant of the admonition to do well as contained in God's word:

> "Do not neglect to do good and to share what you have, for such sacrifices are pleasing to God."
>
> Hebrews 13:16
>
> "Whoever is generous to the poor lends to the Lord, and he will repay him for his deed."
>
> Proverbs 19:17

God loves all people and does not want anyone to perish. God's eyes roam all over throughout the whole earth to watch and find people who fear God and whose hearts are inclined toward him (2 Chronicles 16:9). He is ever eager to pursue man and offer his love and forgiveness to anyone who does works of mercy and generosity to others in need, out of a humble and compassionate heart.

Such was the case of Cornelius, a Roman centurion, whom we read about in Acts 10:1–33. Scripture says that this gentile

Good Works that Lead to God

(non-Jew) was a devout man who feared God, generously gave alms to people, and prayed constantly to God. The Lord acknowledged and assured Cornelius that his prayers and his alms have ascended as a memorial before God. God made a way for Cornelius to hear the gospel. He arranged for Cornelius and Peter the apostle to meet up, so Peter can share the gospel to Cornelius and his entire household. This led Peter to remark, "Truly I understand that God shows no partiality, but in every nation anyone who fears him and does what is right is acceptable to him" (Acts 10:34–35).

The Parable of the Good Samaritan (Luke 10:25–37) is another example of a man doing good works that pleased God, even though he does not belong to God's chosen people. In the story, we see a man who was mugged, stripped, beaten, and left half dead on the road by robbers. A priest saw the man but stayed on the other side and went past him. A Levite, known as worship minister in the Jewish temple, also saw the beaten man but ignored him. Then came a Samaritan who belonged to a community of people who were despised, hated, and considered unclean by the Jewish people back then. This loathed Samaritan went out of his way and spent his own resources to care for the helpless man, "But a Samaritan, as he journeyed, came to where he was, and when he saw him, he had compassion. He went to him and bound up his wounds, pouring oil and wine. Then he set him on his own animal and brought him to an inn and took care of him" (Luke 10:33–34). Jesus asked his disciples who among the three proved to be a neighbor to the helpless man. In this story, Jesus saw the compassionate heart of the Samaritan. He admonished his disciples to do likewise.

In the stories of Cornelius and the Samaritan man, both considered outcast and unregenerate in the eyes of the then larger Jewish society, Jesus compels us to see how godly fear and compassion ought to play out in real life conduct and behavior. No matter what society says about us, no matter our cultural or denominational affiliations, God discerns the attitude of our heart and the actions that emanate from it. Cornelius and the Samaritan man demonstrate for us how godly fear and acts of mercy lead us to Jesus and give us the opportunity to respond to his offer of salvation and eternal life with God.

Part III: The Attributes of a Good God—Biblical Perspective

Today in our contemporary world, it matters less whether each of us is a professing Christian believer, Catholic, Protestant, Methodist, or Baptist—we are all called to be Christ followers, being transformed and perfected to be like Christ. God alone knows who among us are the true worshippers and believers. He alone knows who among us are truly repentant, yielded, and transformed in Christ.

Let us never forget the futility of using good works from a self-righteous heart to earn salvation and eternal life. At the same time, let us be reminded and encouraged that man's good deeds are not remiss from God when done out of a heart and will that submit to God in holy fear, that seek to glorify God, and follow after him.

CHAPTER 20

The Key Attributes of God

To better understand the goodness of God, let us consider some key attributes that are inherent in him. God is immutable; he never ever changes. Unlike man, God is always right in everything he does. God is steadfast in his holiness, justice, mercy, and love.

GOD IS HOLY

The word *holy* is defined as exalted or worthy of complete devotion; holy is one who is perfect in goodness and righteousness.

In the bible, the word holy is mentioned 431 times in the Old Testament. In the New Testament, holy is found 180 times. This shows the high valuation that God imputes on holiness. We bow down to a holy God. God's holiness is like the blinding brightness of the sun to which man cannot look directly. God's pure and undefiled holiness is the reason why he told Moses in Exodus 33:20 (NKJV), "You cannot see My face; for no man shall see Me, and live."

The Hebrew word for holy is *qodesh* which means apartness, sacredness, or separateness. So when we say God is holy, it means God is set apart or separate from his creation. God is totally different from man, he is supremely above man, and he is holy.

In Greek, the word for holy is *hagios* which means pure, morally blameless, or set apart for holy use. Believers are called to be holy just as God is holy. Believers are to be set apart from this sinful world.

Part III: The Attributes of a Good God—Biblical Perspective

The holy God cannot be entangled with anything that is impure. God's holiness demands the absence of darkness and evil. He will not tolerate a person who chooses to persist in wickedness and sin. There is no gray area with God. It is expedient for God to judge justly in order to purge and banish wickedness from his holy presence.

Without holiness, no one will see the Lord (Hebrews 12:14). And separated from the Lord, man can never be holy. Left alone with our sinful nature, however firm and resolute our aspiration to flee, we can never outrun the wily and untrustworthy ways of this world. We will always find ourselves stumbling or compromising with the fallen world, whether openly or secretly. The heart of man without Christ is deceitful (Jeremiah 17:9).

GOD IS JUST

God is just and righteous in all his ways. Jesus provides a striking proof of this when he says about God the Father, "For he makes his sun rise on the evil and on the good, and sends rain on the just and on the unjust" (Matthew 5:45). In the provision of his blessings, God makes no distinction between the evil and the righteous. Yes, the bible talks about the day of the Lord, when God's purposes for this world will be fulfilled, and every wrong will be repaid in full and made right. But until then, God graciously gives good things even to those who go against him, hoping that the wayward would turn to him while there is still time.

God's justice is applied when there is transgression of his laws. God's word says that "the wages of sin is death" (Romans 6:23). Death ultimately means separation from the presence of God. The holy and righteous God cannot co-exist with sinful man, hence there is no other recourse but for God to mete out death for sinners. There is always a consequence to be suffered for wrongdoing. There is no small or big, venial or mortal sin; there is only the presence or absence of sin. As James 2:10 (NKJV) says, "For whoever shall keep the whole law, and yet stumble in one point, he is guilty of all."

The bible teaches that God repays man according to his work and rewards him according to his way (Job 34:11). Surely God can never be wrong nor unjust because righteousness and justice are the foundation of his rule. He shall judge the world, nations, and peoples in uprightness.

As a just God, there is no partiality in his dealings with man. As Zephaniah 3:5 (NKJV) says, "Every morning he brings his justice to light . . . But the unjust knows no shame." Many go about parading their good deeds in public yet keep on defrauding others with dishonest scales. They are proud about their charitable works yet see nothing shameful in tweaking their business books or ledgers to keep money in their pockets. A just God sees everything that man does and never tolerates dishonesty in all forms.

GOD IS MERCIFUL

God is generally acknowledged by man to be merciful more than just. Sinners who believe in a forgiving God count on his mercy again and again. They keep sinning, thinking that God will forgive them anyway. Many take the mercy of God for granted. They consider it as a license to continue living the way they see fit, without serious regard for the teachings and instructions given by the Lord.

God's mercy must not be taken as synonymous with tolerance of wrongdoing. Mercy does not give excuses for man's sinful actions. What parent would shield her child and make excuses to authorities, even if the child bullied or physically injured a classmate in school? What sort of police officer would look the other way and allow an illegal drug peddler to escape because he is a friend? These are man-made ideation of love and mercy which man blindly attributes as God's. God's mercy does not condone man's moral failure; neither does it contradict nor overlook the teachings put down for us in God's word.

Far above the defiled and flawed understanding of God's mercy that many hold, how then does true biblical mercy look like? The mercy of God is intertwined with the love of God—it is deep, long-suffering, compassionate, and forgiving. His mercy is also about disciplining, giving second chances, and starting over with a clean slate. It justifiably requires men to repent and turn away from their wrongdoing or wicked ways. Because God so loves us, out of his great mercy, he does not even give what our many iniquities and transgressions deserve (Psalm 103:10).

Not so with man. Many in the world see mercy or overlooking offense as a form of weakness. To be a winner in today's hypercompetitive world, people are taught to learn to work the system and see things eye for an eye. If somebody slaps you in the face, don't just sit around; you must find a way to hit back, harder if you can. We may be the most loving person, but when we are hurt, it is so hard not to take offense. We say we can forgive but we will never forget. We are prone to keep a record of offenses by other people, so we can conveniently accuse or gloat over them at some future time and avenge the score.

How vastly different are the words and ways of God. Hebrews 8:12 (NKJV) says, "For I will be merciful to their unrighteousness, and their sins and their lawless deeds I will remember no more." Ephesians 2:4–5 (NKJV) declares, "But God, who is rich in mercy, because of His great love with which He loved us, even when we were dead in trespasses, made us alive together with Christ (by grace you have been saved), ..."

GOD IS LOVE

The word *love* in Greek is defined in four ways:[1]

- *Storge*—means familial love which describes the natural bond or instinctual affection between two persons, as love between parent and offspring.
- *Phileo*—is a type of non-romantic attraction, respect, and love between friends and family members. Brotherly love is its common term. It grows when both persons share the same values and principles in life.
- *Eros*—refers to the sensual or passionate love which drives two people to engage in physical sexual intimacy. Eros may occur

---

1. Chapman, "4 Types of Love (Agape, Phileo and . . .)."

within or outside the bond of marriage. The term erotic was rooted in this eros word.

- *Agape*—is a Greco-Christian term referring to love as demonstrated by the God of the bible. Agape is synonymous with unconditional love. It is the love that Jesus Christ pours out for human beings. Christians are taught that agape love is the highest type of love. It is willing the highest good of a person, regardless of how the person behaves toward you as the giver of the agape love.

Jesus points out, "Anyone who does not love does not know God, because God is love. In this the love of God was made manifest among us, that God sent his only Son into the world, so that we might live through him. In this is love, not that we have loved God but that he loved us and sent his Son to be the propitiation for our sins" (1 John 4:8–10).

God's goodness springs from his intrinsic and all-encompassing agape love. His love is not dependent on or ruled upon by external circumstance, temperament, or behavior of the beneficiary. God's love is enduring and does not fade with time. It is constant, persistent, and steadfast.

God loves man even when he goes astray and wanders away from him. The bible is full of remarkable, true to life stories demonstrating God's boundless love, how he took the initiative and pursued men who were rebellious and disobedient to him. Think of Jonah, Hosea and Gomer, and Saul the persecutor who became Paul the apostle. God goes after men and women with whatever means he chooses, be it a fish or disrupting life circumstances, in order to draw them back to him. There is no other God like this, who humbly stoops down and reaches out to flawed and wayward people, to complete his work in and through them. This very same love of God continues to pursue mankind today. Says Romans 5:8, "But God shows his love for us in that while we were still sinners, Christ died for us."

Man, on the other hand, is capable of familial, filial, and erotic love, but conspicuously falls short on the highest agape form of

Part III: The Attributes of a Good God—Biblical Perspective

love. Without God's love as the foundation, man's love for another human being is as unstable as his feelings or emotions.

In today's world, love is loosely defined or practiced by men. Even same sex marriage is now widely accepted and celebrated as a sacred consummation of love. Within both the Christian and non-Christian communities today, there are those who hold the view that heterosexual relations or marriage is not the only sanctioned expression of love. Many conceive that God must look favorably upon same sex relations, since proponents say that this is part of the natural order of things, some individuals are born this way, and they do it out of love.

But what does God's word say about this? We believe that the bible is categorically plain and clear that God created man from the beginning to be male and female, and that sex is intended by God as an expression of love to be enjoyed within the sanctity of marriage between husband and wife.

We share the view held by the Focus on the Family, in their published article "Biblical Perspective on Homosexuality and Same-Sex Marriage":

> "Further, we are convinced that the Bible leaves no room whatsoever for confusion or ambiguity where homosexual behavior is concerned. The Scripture both explicitly and implicitly regards it as falling outside of God's intention in creating man and woman as sexual beings who bear His image as male and female."[2]
>
> "You shall not lie with a male as with a woman; it is an abomination."
>
> Leviticus 18:22
>
> "He answered, 'Have you not read that he who created them from the beginning made them male and female.'"
>
> Matthew 19:4
>
> "Or do you not know that the unrighteous will not inherit the kingdom of God? Do not be deceived: neither the sexually immoral, nor idolaters, nor adulterers, nor

---

2. "Biblical Perspective on Homosexuality and Same-Sex Marriage," Focus on the Family.

men who practice homosexuality, nor thieves . . . will inherit the kingdom of God."

1 Corinthians 6:9-10

Even so, many government and business entities, mass media platforms (TV, movies, radio, print), and social media sites across the world have recognized and legitimized same sex practice as a basic right, championing how far society has supposedly progressed and achieved equality by embracing this cause. Advocates have consolidated the issues of morality in general with the right to autonomy, whereby one need not give account of himself to anybody. Man can do whatever he wants, whenever he wants, with whomever he wants. Much of the world today has elevated same sex practice as a social advocacy worthy of dignity and pride. To support this movement is to be seen as welcoming or inclusive, never mind if it excludes, nullifies, and defies the admonition contained in the word of God.

We recognize that this is a sensitive subject for many. There are multiple facets to this, as it involves not just sexuality, but also one's identity and relationships. Difficult as it may be, "the love of Christ compels us" (2 Corinthians 5:14, NKJV) as authors to mention God's truth firmly but graciously, and to engage in "speaking the truth in love" (Ephesians 4:15). It is immensely important for us to state that our heart is not to shame, condemn, or reject people who support, practice, or experience this kind of affection. It is with genuine concern for one's spiritual well-being that we are pointing this out.

Again, to quote Focus on the Family's "Biblical Perspective on Homosexuality and Same-Sex Marriage":

> "There is no place for hatred, hurtful comments, or other forms of rejection toward those who experience same-sex attraction or identify themselves as gay, lesbian or bisexual. Because we humans are made in the image of God, Jesus teaches us to regard all humanity as having inherent value, worth and dignity—including those affirming or adopting labels or behaviors which we believe the Bible associates with sexual sin. The priority of

love for the Christian is unquestionable, and the cause of love is advanced by telling the truth with grace and compassion."[3]

As Christians, we come alongside individuals who identify with the LGBTQ community, especially since we personally know some within our own circles of family and friends. We love them, the way our Lord Jesus loves them, but not the sin which grieves the heart of God. We believe that it is beneficial for any caring church to prayerfully hold conversations together with our LGBTQ friends, listen to their stories, and make evident the love of Jesus to them in every opportunity. With God's love as motivation, let's study the heart of God concerning these things, and reach out to the point of their readiness to consider the truth from the Lord. We all have sinned and fallen short, but God continues to love each of us deeply and unreservedly. God stands ready to receive and restore anybody who turns to him in repentance and faith.

We leave this subject with the following words from author and host Becket Cook, who is among the few remaining voices who speak out God's grace and truth on this issue:

> "It may seem loving to affirm our gay friends or relatives, but it is actually quite the opposite. With eternity at stake, the most loving thing we can do as Christians is to tell them the truth that, yes, homosexual behavior is a sin, but that forgiveness and mercy can be found in Jesus Christ."[4]

In the same vein, pregnancy out of wedlock and killing of babies through legalized abortion have become so commonplace, it no longer shocks or surprises many people today. Experimental relationships like living-in has also become widely acceptable. Many consider this as the de facto way to test or try out human love and sexual compatibility with no commitment, allowing for a convenient way out in case the trial relationship does not work. On the contrary, a man or woman who chooses to stay chaste before

3. "Biblical Perspective on Homosexuality . . . ," Focus on the Family.
4. Cook, "How to Love Your LGBT Neighbor During Pride Month (and Every Month)."

marriage is typically subjected to ridicule, oftentimes portrayed as a joke or a laughingstock by contemporary media entertainment. The world has so twisted the definition of God's love upside down, customarily redefining lust as love. Cultural norms today have come to define and express love in a way that does not only tolerate sin, but also embraces and celebrates sin.

God's love is in stark contrast with human love. Amazingly so, despite man's flagrant rebellion and opposition, God does not withhold his love. The Lord patiently persists to make known both his promises and warnings to both the repentant and the unrepentant, in the hope that many will recognize their errant beliefs or ways and turn back to God. But do not for a moment think that he is willing to overlook our sins because he loves us. Let us not mistake God's love for tolerance of sin. God loves us but also commands us to sin no more.

PART IV

No One is Good, All Have Sinned

CHAPTER 21

The Sinful Nature of Man

As established in the previous chapter, the only way we can know true goodness is by acquiring a biblical understanding of the one true living God. God is holy, just, infinitely merciful, and loving—there is not a tint or shade of sin in him. God is pure, undefiled, and cannot tolerate sin. God abhors sin because it goes against his nature and character as the perfect Holy One.

Unless we accept this truth, and see ourselves in light of God's holiness, our strivings toward goodness will always fall short before God. Man's perception of good and God's measure of goodness are poles apart. Unless we understand how contradictory our perception of who is good and who qualifies for eternal life, with the goodness that God accepts and requires, there is no hope for man. There is hope only because God himself provided hope in the person of his son Jesus.

From the beginning of time, in the Genesis account in the bible, God created man for his good pleasure. Everything that God created is good. And man is God's creation, therefore man is good. Genesis 1:31 (NKJV) says, "Then God saw everything that He had made, and indeed it was very good . . . ."

Even King David attests in Psalm 139:14, "I praise you, for I am fearfully and wonderfully made. Wonderful are your works; my soul knows it very well." If man was created good and wonderful, what led him to sin and fall out of God's favor? According

Part IV: No One is Good, All Have Sinned

to Scripture, the root of the problem began when Adam and Eve disobeyed God's expressed command. When tempted by Satan who appeared in the form of a snake in the Garden of Eden, Adam and Eve succumbed and fell into the sin of pride and rebellion. They willfully disobeyed God who told them not to eat from the fruit of the tree of the knowledge of good and evil, or they will die. Satan deceived Eve by saying they will not die. He backed this up with the falsehood that God did not want them to eat of the forbidden tree because if they did, they would be like God.

Genesis 3:6–7 reads, "So when the woman saw that the tree was good for food, and that it was a delight to the eyes, and that the tree was to be desired to make one wise, she took of its fruit and ate, and she also gave some to her husband who was with her, and he ate. Then the eyes of both were opened, and they knew that they were naked. And they sewed fig leaves together and made themselves loincloths."

When Adam and Eve ate the fruit of the forbidden tree, it essentially created a breach in their covenantal relationship or trust agreement with God. Adam's and Eve's action cast doubt and disbelief on the love and goodness that God lavished on them. It signified an intent to be independent from God and an ambition to become like God. Man's willful disobedience and defiance are deeply dishonoring and hurtful towards God. It impaired the good and noble purposes that God intended and designed for his created beings.

Consequently, God banished Adam and Eve from his presence. They forfeited what was supposed to be an abundant life with full unmitigated access to God, and all the blessings that go with it. They lost the covering of moral purity that God placed on them. Malice entered as their minds became depraved and skewed. Their spirit became seared and separated from God. Their physical bodies were subjected to toil, weakness, decay, and death. After the fall, all men have become dead in sin and iniquity.

Notice what Adam and Eve did to cover their nakedness—they sewed fig leaves to clothe themselves. This was man's first attempt to cover up sin and bridge his way back to fellowship with God. This was fallen man's self-efforts to reconcile with the holy God, a foreshadow of the many outward ceremonial forms and externalism that man continues to do as a way to bridge the gap and attempt to connect with his Creator.

The desire in man to do good exists since God instilled in him the ability to know what is right and wrong through his conscience. Most of the time, however, what man knows as good, he doesn't do. He may start right, but he always ends up missing the mark of God's righteousness. As man struggles with temptations, he wittingly or unwittingly ends up choosing wrong and committing sin. His conscience eventually becomes dulled, and falling into sin becomes a habit, a lifestyle. The apostle Paul succinctly expressed this inner conflict in man in Romans 7:15–17, "For I do not understand my own actions. For I do not do what I want, but I do the very thing I hate. Now if I do what I do not want, I agree with the law, that it is good. So now it is no longer I who do it, but sin that dwells within me." We inherited a sinful nature from Adam and Eve after their fall. We don't want to do what is wrong, but we do it anyway because sin has put our hearts in bondage. We become slaves to what controls us.

Countless people in the world today consider truth relative. What is right for you may be wrong for me, what is right for me may be wrong for you. And the world today accepts this to be perfectly okay. The secular world twists, if not disregards, biblical truths. We now live in the so-called Post Truth era, where absolute truth no longer exists.

Human philosophies, man-made religions, and ideologies held captive man's mind and conformed him to the ways of the world. The fallen man thinks that it is within his power, his self-will, his own strength, and abilities to make and build a good life, regardless of and independent of God. The sophistication and lure of worldly philosophies and beliefs have so enamored men that many endorse these views to be life-changing, a balm for the soul in this stressful world. The more pervasive ones include religious formalism, materialism, humanism, post-modernism, dualism, expressive individualism, liberalism, the new age spirituality, occultism, superstitions, feng shui, yoga, yin and yang. Many find these beliefs not only practicable but also fashionable, a trendy and blissful way to live life. Taken at face value, many of these philosophies appear harmless and charmingly appealing. However, a careful examination of them and the doctrines they espouse reveal a reliance on the self and not on God. Foundationally, these schools of thought do not acknowledge God. Some even contradict God's truths as taught in Scripture. The ideological lines have been so cleverly blurred that even well-meaning Christians may miss it.

CHAPTER 22

The Deceptive Philosophies of the World

Many today embrace deceptive, worldly philosophies and wear them like godly, spiritual clothing. Many professed followers of Christ adhere and practice the tenets of these humanistic philosophies, as shown in the way they think and make everyday life decisions. If we are not grounded in biblical truths, and if we do not exercise spiritual discernment, we will be lost in the self-focused ways of the world. If we do not have the appetite to learn and follow the ways of Christ as taught in the bible, we will be easily swayed, manipulated, and deceived. For instance, one may read and teach the word of God, but at the same time dabble in fortune-telling, horoscope, and feng shui. Many have impressive head knowledge of the bible and can easily quote biblical texts, only to take God's word out of context and justify self-serving deeds.

"For as he thinks in his heart, so is he" counsels Proverbs 23:7 (NKJV). As William "Winkie" Pratney, author of *Youth Aflame: A Manual for Discipleship*, puts it:

> "An idea is a spark—a spark that can fire a world. The way you think is the way you will live. All worldly philosophies have serious weaknesses and dangerous

Part IV: No One is Good, All Have Sinned

consequences when a life is based on them. How much of the world's ideas run your life?"[1]

All this is to say that the humanistic and ungodly worldviews that are popularly consumed by many in the mainstream world, are devised by the sly machinations and maneuverings of the evil one. Remember that Satan himself knows the bible and can readily quote Scripture, like when he tempted Jesus multiple times to sin; yet he remained unconverted and opposed to God. Satan is a defeated foe, but he is working double time to seduce many in the world into rebellion against God. Let us examine how he uses some of these worldviews and ideologies to deceive, corrupt, and manipulate men.

RELIGIOUS FORMALISM—FAITH IN TRADITION

This philosophy hinders God from drawing people to him and transforming them to becoming the kingdom people he intended them to be. Religious formalism ignores God's instruction for people to worship him in spirit and truth as the bible prescribes. It leads man to put more premium on performing religious exercises, without necessarily gaining a real understanding of how lost we are without Christ and how gravely dependent we are to him. When engaging in certain religious rites or duties, there is the propensity for man to think that he earns forgiveness or merits favors/rewards, and so secures his soul. This is a grave mistake and contradicts Scripture. Empty moral externalism, without the conviction of our utter sinfulness and the need for Christ to forgive and rescue us, does not please God. Jesus had numerous confrontations with the religious formalists during his earthly life, and he sharply rebuked them for their hypocrisy, empty righteousness, and unbelief.

Man is naturally captivated and engrossed with the flurry of activities of everyday earthly living—family, school, work, business, social engagements, recreation. He has little interest and time, if any, for sitting still before God, praying, and studying God's word. He is content doing the things of God during church service or

---

1. Pratney, *Youth Aflame*, 23.

prayer meetings; fellowship with God is done while inside the church building. He is prone to believe that his soul is safe as long as he keeps his religious obligations. Sunday church has little or nothing to do with how he conducts himself for the rest of the week. Once the obligation is done, Jesus is set aside until the next church service.

In Mark 7:6–9, Jesus rebuked this traditionalism by calling out the Pharisees and teachers of the law, "And he said to them, 'Well did Isaiah prophesy of you hypocrites, as it is written, 'This people honors me with their lips, but their heart is far from me; in vain do they worship me, teaching as doctrines the commandments of men.' You leave the commandment of God and hold to the tradition of men.' And he said to them, 'You have a fine way of rejecting the commandment of God in order to establish your tradition!'"

Religion is oftentimes esteemed by man as a substitute for God. It has become man's way of reaching out to his own idea of a god, not the God of the bible. True Christianity is not a religion, but rather a personal friendship with Jesus. It requires intentionality on man's part to know him and spend quality time with him, like the friendships we have with people. Jesus makes it perfectly clear, "I am the way, and the truth, and the life. No one comes to the Father except through me" (John 14:6). Religion is not the way to eternal life; Jesus is. This is what the Lord Jesus means when he presents himself as the gate, the door (John 10:9). We can never get to heaven without entering by him. Outwardly clinging to a religion is man's way, not God's way.

The Lord is not like the pagan gods, fashioned with wood, metal, or stone. Today, many still bow down to lifeless idols the way the Babylonians, Romans, and Greeks did. Pagans worship their god statues like Baal, Ashtoreth, Ammon, Molech, Venus, Artemis, Zeus, Caesar Emperor, Athena, Buddha, and Mohammad. In some cultures, people even worship their dead ancestors, nature, and animal gods. Religious people who bow down to wooden or stone statues of Jesus, Mary, and other saints are doing the same thing that pagans do. A pagan is defined as a person who worships man-made gods or goddesses, the earth, or even nature.

Part IV: No One is Good, All Have Sinned

In worshiping like pagans do, sincere believers unknowingly dishonor the one true living God who categorically directed his followers to worship him in spirit and truth. The instruction given by God not to worship him with man-made graven images is explicit and clear. Hear the heart of God in his own words:

> "You shall not make for yourself a carved image—any likeness of anything that is in heaven above, or that is in the earth beneath, or that is in the water under the earth; you shall not bow down to them nor serve them. For I, the Lord your God, am a jealous God, visiting the iniquity of the fathers upon the children to the third and fourth generations of those who hate Me, but showing mercy to thousands, to those who love Me and keep My commandments."
>
> Exodus 20:4-6 (NKJV)
>
> "What profit is an idol when its maker has shaped it, a metal image, a teacher of lies? For its maker trusts in his own creation when he makes speechless idols! Woe to him who says to a wooden thing, Awake; to a silent stone, Arise! Can this teach? Behold, it is overlaid with gold and silver, and there is no breath at all in it."
>
> Habakkuk 2:18-19

Many well-meaning people bow down and pray to dead saints or to icons like Mary the earthly mother of Jesus, or even the Pope, and dead loved ones. This is not biblical, and it contradicts God. The word of God does not teach that Mary is an intermediary between Jesus and man, nor does it commend the reciting of repetitive prayers and petitions to saints or martyrs in the faith. God directs people to turn to him and be saved; he alone can do it and there is no other (Isaiah 45:22).

If the Blessed Virgin Mary was alive today, she would most likely be disheartened and anguished when she sees people pray to her, bow down to her, and venerate her in pedestals and religious parades. A most humble and devoted servant of God, Mary exalted the Lord, not herself, in her prayer and praise song. Like other women of faith in the bible who fervently sought and prayed to the one true God, Mary acknowledged herself to be a sinner needing a savior by calling the Lord "my Savior" in her own words. As Luke 1:46–48 records, "And Mary said, 'My soul magnifies the Lord, and my spirit rejoices in God my Savior, for he has looked on the humble estate of his servant.'" Now if Mary, chosen and called to become the earthly mother of Jesus, humbly accepted her need for forgiveness and called God her Savior, how much more should we? Evidently Mary knew the Scriptures; how she must have saturated her mind and heart with the word of God. Bible scholars believe that Mary spent substantial time reading and memorizing scriptures since her praise song contains allusions to the Old Testament (the Scripture during her time).

Mary, in her humility, would be grieved to see believers praying to her and parading her image. As a Jew, the Virgin Mary knew and obeyed God's command not to bow down to images or idols, as instructed in Old Testament Scriptures. She would not dare offend the God she loved by getting the glory which she knew is for Jesus and Jesus alone. She would most certainly point believers to pray directly to Jesus, who is the great High Priest and intercessor to the Father.

God did not call Mary nor the apostles nor the canonized saints to forever intercede for the living ones, to petition Jesus for men. Like us, these people of faith had struggles and infirmities; but it is God Almighty who equips the people who humbly submit to his calling. It was not by their own power that they overcame and accomplished things for God, but on account of the strength and grace given to them by God. Mary and the apostles clearly knew this, as evidenced by the numerous descriptive records in the bible where they magnified the Lord and owed everything they came to be to the God their Savior. They rightfully saw their place as dutiful servants of the Lord, nothing less and nothing more (Luke 17:10). Why many today elevate them to the point of idolatry must arise from a lack of Scripture-based knowledge and understanding of who Mary and the apostles really were, and how they obeyed the God they loved.

Also like us, Mary, the apostles, and the canonized saints were mere mortals with physical bodies, who have since died. They do not have a divine nature and they are not omnipresent like God. We cannot pray to dead mortal people, no matter how godly they were in their lifetime. Why consult the dead on behalf of the living (Isaiah 8:19)? The Lord commanded us to seek guidance directly from him (1 Chronicles 10:13–14). The word of God admonishes Christians not to seek out or talk to dead people, or else render themselves unclean and dishonorable before his eyes (Leviticus 19:31). How can the living ones even pray to dead saints? Searching by the Scriptures, not only does this practice not achieve anything, but it also contradicts God's directive and corrupts our relationship with him.

We must carefully examine ourselves against falling into the subtle sin of false religious zeal, thinking that we are performing acceptable service to God, when in truth we are committing the deadly sin of praying to idols. Only the Lord Jesus, who is both fully God and fully man, having been resurrected to life and witnessed by many to be alive, can hear our prayers. We, who are still living, are the ones called to be intercessors and prayer warriors for one another, in the name of Jesus. Mary was most likely a prayerful intercessor during her lifetime. However, upon her assumption to heaven, with the death of her mortal and physical body, she could no longer be an intercessor.

Again, this book does not intend to pass judgment on people who love and adore Mary, the mother of Jesus. As Christians, we too love Mary for she is without question a virtuous woman of God. Along with the apostles and the many Christian disciples who were martyred for the Lord, we look up to Mary as a saint to emulate. The humble, servant heart of Mary towards God, along with her love of God's word and obedience to it, is what should spur us to also become true followers of Christ.

Idolatry is the worship of an idol in place of God, be it a physical image, a person, or any man-made construct. It is looking up to or beholding another entity, not sanctioned by God, to perform or meet a need within us. God does not want to be worshipped like any other created, man-made idol. God the creator of all is alive; we worship a living God. He is spirit and he cannot be contained; even the heaven and the highest heaven cannot contain him (1 Kings

8:27). Containing our Almighty Creator God in any object form belittles him and implies failure or refusal to submit to his authority. We betray God and we harm our relationship with him if we turn our eyes away from him and behold other man-made entity in our hearts. Idolatry is a grievous sin against God since pride is at the root of it. It is man bowing to something that he creates on his own, apart and separate from God's holiness.

The word of God teaches true worship to Jesus in this way, "God is spirit, and those who worship him must worship in spirit and truth" (John 4:24). Worshipping God in any other way than this is grievous before his eyes. The apostle Paul poses this challenge to those who consider themselves to be true children of God, "Being then God's offspring, we ought not to think that the divine being is like gold or silver or stone, an image formed by the art and imagination of man. The times of ignorance God overlooked, but now he commands all people everywhere to repent" (Acts 17:29–30).

MATERIALISM—FAITH IN POSSESSIONS AND THINGS

Materialism is a philosophy that believes all reality consist of matter and energy. It is a mindset that looks at the material world to experience reality and rejects immaterial entities like souls or spirits. It is a belief that is grounded on what one sees, hears, touches, smells, and tastes. Things that stimulate the brain create the inner self reality.

The world today is embroiled in going after earthly things that satisfy the physical senses. Without realizing it, many good people anchor their self-worth and security on their ability to create wealth and acquire tangible things. Contentment is derived in accumulating stuff such as houses, cars, jewelries, designer bags, or electronic gadgets. Their valuation and estimation of people is colored by a person's success in life, his social status and influence, bank accounts, and assets. Their dreams for their children have everything to do with scholastic and material gains, and little or even nothing to do with accomplishing things for God.

Part IV: No One is Good, All Have Sinned

It may do us well to test the inclination of our hearts if we are yet ensnared in the web of materialism. How does the quality of our prayer time compare with the time we spend at work or in our business? What legacy are we looking to leave our kids? Are we concerned at all with their spiritual welfare, or is it enough that we hand them our accumulated things and they shall be secure? Do we delight in spending time with God and his Word, as much as we enjoy taking vacations in the company of family and friends? Or do all these questions concerning God and spending time with him sound strange since they are not really a part of our daily routine?

Let's not misunderstand, God does not want his people to lack anything. The bible prescribes man to labor diligently and to manage his resources well so that he will "be dependent on no one" (1 Thessalonians 4:11–12). What Scripture identifies as the root of all evil is not money or material things per se, but the love and insatiable pursuit of it (1 Timothy 6:10). We all know that life in general—shelter, education, healthcare, retirement—is easier when we have money or the means for it. This is why many have come to depend on the acquisition of wealth for security. Considering our fervor to create and enjoy wealth, do we have the same if not greater longing to become rich toward God? (Luke 12:20-21; 1 Timothy 6:17-19)

It is well to be reminded of Jesus' wealth portfolio advice, which in all probability is something we will never hear from investment asset managers today, "Do not lay up for yourselves treasures on earth, where moth and rust destroy and where thieves break in and steal, but lay up for yourselves treasures in heaven, where neither moth nor rust destroys and where thieves do not break in and steal. For where your treasure is, there your heart will be also" (Matthew 6:19–21). Let us be on guard lest we fall into a false sense of self-sufficiency. When we come to the end of all things, pursuing richness in Christ and relying on him, not on ourselves and our possessions, would have been worth it all; for those who choose him will not be put to shame (Joel 2:27; 1 Peter 2:6).

More than physical things, materialism also defines our moral propensities, loyalty, and affiliations. The Lord Jesus says in Luke 16:13, "No servant can serve two masters, for either he will hate the one and love the other, or he will be devoted to the one and despise the other. You cannot serve God and money." Many good people counter and say with confidence that materialism is not an issue with them at all because they are generous with their possessions. But lest we mix up one with the other, generous giving and sacrificial giving are two different things (Mark 12:41–44). Sin also encroaches when people take pride in what they share with others. In other cases, good people succumb to the entrapment and temptations associated with the ownership of things, like the sins of envy, covetousness, greed, corruption, pride, arrogance, quarrels and disputes, theft, and robbery. It may also do us well to conduct a self-check if we take pride in the company of the people of God, as much as we take honor and pleasure in the company of materially rich and well-connected friends.

Materialism denies God the honor that is due him—to be desired, exalted, and loved above all. God after all is the creator of all things. Everything comes from God, including silver and gold. So why should man set him aside who is the source of it all? May it never be true of us what the apostle Paul said of Demas, his co-worker in ministry, "For Demas, in love with this present world, has deserted me and gone to Thessalonica" (2 Timothy 4:10).

HUMANISM—FAITH IN MAN

Humanism is a philosophy that underscores the value or worth of human beings, individually and collectively. It elevates mankind as solely responsible for progress, development, and betterment in this world. Humanist beliefs are centered on man's needs, interests, and abilities. Philanthropy or humanitarian benevolence is emphasized. To understand the world, humanists look to science. Humanists uphold reason, ethics, socio-economic justice, and equality as the basis for morality, decision making, and progress. Dogma and the supernatural have no place in the humanist worldview. All knowledge and moral standards are based on human experience and rational thinking. God is out of the picture in humanism. The idea of God as the source of revealed knowledge is flatly rejected.

Part IV: No One is Good, All Have Sinned

In this light, if you consider the humanistic view on good works and benevolent acts toward others, many will conclude that humanists are indeed good people. However, the contention here again is that the *self* is magnified, not *God*.

People who hold this belief system take pride in feeling good about themselves every time they help others in commendable ways. They are convinced that it is within man's power to make this world a better place by strongly advocating for social justice, social reforms, equality, diversity, and inclusivity. Behind this progressive and philanthropic worldview, however, lies the faulty presumption that man is all-sufficient, all-mighty, and all-knowing, completely capable to live an upright life without need for God.

To be sure, there is nothing wrong in feeding the poor or helping the marginalized in society. Humanitarian works are vital and good in and of itself. Even Scripture encourages the followers of Jesus to do good.

> "In the same way, let your light shine before others, so that they may see your good works and give glory to your Father who is in heaven."
>
> Matthew 5:16
>
> "And let us consider how to stir up one another to love and good works."
>
> Hebrews 10:24

What makes this worldview, which is all about man doing good works, unacceptable in God's eyes? We need to comprehend that the Lord looks beyond the outward deeds of man. What matters to him is the heart attitude, intent, and motivation behind the deed.

In the words of pastor and author A.W. Tozer:

> "The purpose of good works isn't to change or save us; rather, it's the demonstration of the change within us."[2]

The Lord knows whether one's good works emanate from a transformed heart that sincerely seeks to obey and glorify God, or are motivated by self-serving interests, e.g., self-glorification,

---

2. Tozer, "The purpose of good works . . . ."

self-preservation, tax write-offs, corporate branding. Humanists do good deeds for the sake of men, not for God's glory. Many people help others either to make themselves look good or to feel good about themselves.

It is difficult for people who hold the humanist worldview to acknowledge themselves as falling short before God, to see themselves as sinners needing a Savior. Why call them sinful when they are the first in line to volunteer, serve the community, and advocate for the marginalized? This is sadly the case when good works become the obstacle or blinders, making people unable to see how God views unregenerate men—sinful and in need of a Savior. Even many professed Christians embrace humanism and applaud distinguished men and women who are generous philanthropists, never mind if they believe in God or not.

POST-MODERNISM—FAITH IN SUBJECTIVE TRUTH AND REALITY

As a philosophy, post-modernism upholds pluralism and relativism. It rejects the idea of absolute truth. Values, truth, morality, politics, education, and reality differ from person to person, culture to culture. All these are based on how a person constructs his own realities and experience. As with the other worldviews, post-modernism is focused on the *self*. Again, God's absolute truths and biblical authority have no place in a post-modernist reality.

People who subscribe to the idea of "my truth, your truth" adhere to a post-modernist view. Truth is relative. There is no objective reality. The idea of pluralism in a post-modernist mind involves the doctrine of multiplicity, meaning there is more than one correct logic. In art, there can be many directions and interpretations at the same time, based on the different artists' points of view. In religion, there is no one true religion, but many true religions based on one's own set of beliefs and values. There are many paths to that one universal concept of God. It is up to each person to construct that path or choose from the many routes that lead to the same destination, whatever that is.

Part IV: No One is Good, All Have Sinned

A great number of professing believers in Christ have also fallen into this post-modernist narrative. Yes, they read the bible, but post-modernist thinkers interpret biblical passages and stories based on their own personal understanding and application to their own life experience and circumstance. They ignore the exegesis of biblical studies and interpretation; meaning, they care less about the analysis of biblical text in its original language, context, and form. A religious post-modernist is only concerned about how the biblical text would affect his personal life in a positive light. He cherry picks bible verses which are relevant to his own good, his own goals, and aspirations.

DUALISM—FAITH IN TWO OPPOSING REALITIES

The doctrine of Dualism posits that everything we perceive or believe can be explained in two fundamental concepts or realities, and these two are separate and opposed to each other. To help understand dualism, contrast it with the belief systems known as Monism and Pluralism. Monism states that every phenomenon we experience essentially comes from one universal reality. On the other hand, Pluralism maintains that there is not just one common reality, nor two sets of reality, but many co-existing realities.

There are different types of dualism put forward by various philosophers throughout the centuries. Among these are the divergent concepts or beliefs in good and evil, mental and physical, mind and body, person and body, fact and value. We shall only briefly discuss here what is called as the "Substance Dualism" worldview, which many scholars and academicians offer as a helpful discourse in understanding the ideological principles behind important issues like abortion, euthanasia, and same sex attraction.

A substance dualist presents a fragmented view of the nature of human being as comprising of two elements—a body and a person. This worldview postulates the "body" to be a separate, physical, and biological entity, distinct from the "person" of the human being. A man can do to the body whatever pleases him, with little or no moral attribution and consequences. For other than the body,

The Deceptive Philosophies of the World

there's a separate entity of the person where the facet of the human being that thinks, feels, reacts, and contributes to the world around him resides. This belief system is also termed as the fact/value split, where the body is the fact and the person is the value.

The fact/value split dichotomy in a way provides impetus to the ideas of subjective reality and secular morality. It offers a framework where the individual can set aside absolute truth by relying on his own valuation system as a person and permits him to perceive the body as an amoral aspect of his humanity. For those who support or believe or engage in this worldview, it helps explain why it's possible to have no dissonance or no feeling of conflict, guilt, or moral responsibility attached to certain manners or situations by which the human body is purposed or subjected. The idea of the biological physical body is not central or relevant to the individual's identity.

Following this philosophy, it becomes possible for an individual to remain faithfully engaged with his church, and at the same time support secular morality, which on many points is diametrically opposed to biblical morality. This worldview permits a believer to sincerely think he is staying true to his faith identity, even as he supports or observes practices that run counter to scriptural precepts.

Scripture is clear on its teaching that God created man with a body, soul, and spirit. Such is the apostle Paul's ending benediction in the book of First Thessalonians:

> "Now may the God of peace himself sanctify you completely, and may your whole spirit and soul and body be kept blameless at the coming of our Lord Jesus Christ. He who calls you is faithful; he will surely do it."
>
> 1 Thessalonians 5:23–24

Notice how Paul admonished believers to surrender all to the authority of Christ, so that he may keep us to himself, and separate us from sin entirely in spirit, soul, and body. We are to be holy in mind, body, and soul; we cannot be holy in mind only but not in body, or vice versa. Paul proceeds to say that though this sanctification process is not easy and may not be within man's capability, assuredly our faithful God who takes care of his own will do it.

May the love of God move us to care for and honor the body, soul, and spirit that he has gifted us with. Christ is not a doctrine or philosophy; he is the son of God who condescended to become a mortal person, suffered an excruciating death on the cross, to redeem man from sin. Our body is not our own; we were bought at a price, and we are called to glorify God in body and in spirit (1 Corinthians 6:19–20).

MARXISM/COMMUNISM/SOCIALISM— FAITH IN MARX

Marxism is a philosophy that kick-started the transformation of society into the political systems of Communism and Socialism. Communism advocates a stateless society which eradicates social classes and promotes identical treatment to all who are considered equal. It espouses revolution to achieve transformation. Many scholars believe that Communism sounds good in theory, but not in practice. Under this system, the government is run solely by the party leaders in power. Ordinary citizens who violate the rules are punished, imprisoned, retrained, disappeared; it is the government who knows and determines what is best for everyone. This philosophy is anti-God and anti-democracy. It is a documented fact that many Christians are detained and persecuted in Communist-run states, where basic liberties are denied. Any opposing political and religious views are quashed and silenced, even punished to death.

Socialism is a political and economic system that is allied with Communism; it socializes the ownership and regulation of production, distribution, and exchange of wealth by workers in the community. On paper, Socialism appears to be compatible with the ideals of democracy and liberty. It claims to promote equality, providing equal access and social service benefits for all. In practice, however, it is also an authoritarian rule by the Head of the Socialist state, much like how the Communist Party Head rules and controls the workers and the people. There is no religious freedom in a socialist state. It is likewise anti-God in practice.

Marxism and Socialism basically deny the value God places on individual man and deny the power of God to change or transform society according to his kingdom truths.

SPIRITISM—FAITH IN FEAR

Spiritism is a philosophy that upholds the belief that dead human beings communicate with the living. It is believed that the spirits of the dead live on and can communicate with those who are alive through a medium called as spiritualist. A medium is a person who can speak to the deceiving spirits of dead persons. He conjures up their spirits to take the medium's body in a trance-like state to speak to the living.

Spiritualists are men who have been tricked by the evil one into supernatural communion with gods and with the souls of dead loved ones. Make no mistake, this is Satanic counterfeit and impersonation. Satan is the father and prince of lies (John 8:44). The word of God warns against the danger of dallying and engaging in this dark occult practice.

> "There shall not be found among you anyone who makes his son or daughter pass through the fire, or one who practices witchcraft, or a soothsayer, or one who interprets omens, or a sorcerer, or one who conjures spells, or a medium, or a spiritist, or one who calls up the dead. For all who do these things are an abomination to the Lord, and because of these abominations the Lord your God drives them out from before you. You shall be blameless before the Lord your God."
>
> Deuteronomy 18:10–13 (NKJV)

Spiritism is involved with the demonic forces behind occult practices. If one opens his soul to occultism, he becomes vulnerable to demonic attacks and possession. The common devices used by spiritualists include the following, many of which have been normalized and trivialized today as exciting phenomena of thrill and adventure:

- Divination techniques with the use of Ching, tarot, or playing cards;
- Fortune telling tools like crystal balls, tea leaves, palmistry;
- Non-Christian sources of guidance and hope like astrology, horoscope, ouija board, and seances;
- Games and entertainment techniques that require a person to give up the conscious control of his mind and will, like transcendental meditation, high level acid music exposure, entertainment hypnosis, religious chants, and use of hallucinogenic drugs.

Close fellowship with God and the faithful study of the warnings and instructions in the word of God are the Christian's best weapons against these deceptions from the wicked one.

NEW AGE PHILOSOPHY—FAITH IN MAN-MADE SPIRITUALITY

The New Age movement is an offshoot of occultism. It emphasizes a person's spirituality or the spiritual authority of the self. It espouses a common belief in various semi-divine, non-human entities like angels and masters with whom human beings can communicate through channeling. Adherents of this New Age movement call themselves spiritual seekers. It has evolved into a hodge-podge of beliefs like reincarnation, transcendental meditation, alternative healing, astrology, psychics, and presence of spiritual energy in physical objects like mountains or trees.

The core view of this philosophy is hinged on this concept—that a New Age of heightened spiritual consciousness and international peace would bring an end to racism, poverty, sickness, hunger, and war. Individuals can have a foretaste of this New Age through spiritual transformation.

Many people who profess to follow Christ may also indulge themselves in Hindu or Chinese philosophies and practices, such as yoga meditation, yin and yang, and the popular feng shui. These are touted to attract good vibrations, positive energies, and good luck

The Deceptive Philosophies of the World

to one's life. Some wear lucky charm bracelets, crucifix necklace, rosary bead bracelets, and even replicas of the physical bible book as amulets or protection from bad luck or harm. People are led to think that if they wear or carry these things, they are protected. This is dangerously false and unbiblical. The deceitful adversary wants to take the eyes and heart of man off the one true living God, who alone can protect and deliver us from harm. The security of our lives is not dependent on luck or any material thing, but on Christ alone.

In this belief system, spirituality is not rooted in the God of the bible. It teaches that oneself, equipped with various man-made tools and techniques, can achieve spirituality. This worldview shuts God out of man's spiritual life.

As the apostle Paul warned the true followers of Christ:

> "Beware lest anyone cheat you through philosophy and empty deceit, according to the tradition of men, according to the basic principles of the world, and not according to Christ."
>
> Colossians 2:8 (NKJV)

Since we were all born spiritually dead and separated from God, we are indeed helpless by ourselves to come out of this despondence. If we desire to reconnect with our Creator God, we must be made spiritually alive. But left on our own, we are powerless to do this.

Who then can reconcile us back to God?

PART V

The Folly of Self-Righteousness

CHAPTER 23

The Vanity of Man-Made Efforts to Holiness

Scripture teaches that no unrighteous thing shall enter the kingdom of heaven. Jesus and his disciples went about preaching the kingdom of God to the Jews first, then to the Gentiles. The key question then is how do we enter and become part of God's kingdom? From the very beginning, men labored to answer this on their own. Relying on their own smarts, and trusting in their own perceived righteousness, men devised their own ways to restore their relationship with God. How these man-made efforts came about can be traced back to the fall of our first parents. We touched on this in the previous chapter, when we went over the biblical account of how Adam and Eve succumbed to Satan's lie and sinned. After willfully disobeying God by eating from the forbidden tree, their eyes were opened, and they saw themselves naked; with shame they sewed fig leaves to cover themselves up. This was man's attempt to remedy the issue of nakedness and shame before God because of sin.

Since all men are born into this sinful condition, nothing much has changed. Most people today continue to live life on their own terms. They fit God in their lives in a way that is most convenient, so as not to disrupt the picture-perfect puzzle of life they have put together and built. As it was with Adam and Eve, many of us also go about doing our own thing, according to our own understanding of what we believe will benefit us and give us a sense of rightness before God.

Mankind continues to rely on his own standards of kindness and good deeds, on account of which he presumes acceptance with God. Man's self-efforts gave rise to the different religions, philosophies, and ideologies as we know them today. But think for a moment, is it truly possible for us to secure our own soul through the work of our hands? Can we bank on our own determination of what God approves, of what will secure us entry to heaven and what will not?

What does man essentially need to do to have eternal life? For those who read Scripture, this question certainly rings familiar. This is the exact same question Jesus was asked in Luke 18:18, "And a ruler asked him, 'Good Teacher, what must I do to inherit eternal life?'"

Indeed, our world today is not lacking in rich young rulers—rich in knowledge and abundant in good works. Many of us are born into the religion of our parents; we do our best to follow the Ten Commandments, live decently, work hard, join ministries, and abide by the law, including God's moral laws. These instill in us a sense that we are somehow eligible to receive God's favor; that God will look upon us approvingly and give us the proverbial pat on the back.

Unfortunately, if we read further to see how the young ruler ended up in the story, we find that all his knowledge of Scripture and his acts of service since he was a boy, did not secure him a sure ticket to heaven. There was something else that possessed the heart of this young man, which hindered him from accepting the invitation of Jesus to go follow him.

Picking up from Luke 18:21–27, the text reads: "And he said, 'All these I have kept from my youth.' When Jesus heard this, he said to him, 'One thing you still lack. Sell all that you have and distribute to the poor, and you will have treasure in heaven; and come, follow me.' But when he heard these things, he became very sad, for he was extremely rich. Jesus, seeing that he had become sad, said, 'How difficult it is for those who have wealth to enter the kingdom of God! For it is easier for a camel to go through the eye of a needle than for a rich person to enter the kingdom of God.' Those who heard it said, 'Then who can be saved?' But he said, 'What is impossible with man is possible with God.'"

For those of us who may think that we are approved of God because of our godly beliefs and deeds, Jesus' words should pose a serious red-light warning. Having religious knowledge and doing righteous works are not enough to save our souls. The Lord reads the inward motives of all who consider themselves Christ followers. He knows exactly why we do the things we do; he knows us better than we know ourselves. The Lord is not impressed with our toils and professions of faith, when in truth our heart is fixed on something else. The secret loves and affections of our hearts are not hidden from God.

When asked to give up the things he has accumulated in life, the young ruler despaired and walked away from Jesus. He couldn't do it. He was torn between his earthly treasure and his obedience to God. When put to the test, the young ruler chose the fleeting things of this world over friendship with Jesus. The young man held tightly to his material somethings, not knowing that when he rejected Jesus, he lost everything. His own sense of righteousness crumbled when confronted by the Lord. His declaration that he kept and obeyed the Ten Commandments was not true after all, because there were other things he loved and treasured more than God.

Knowing God takes more than zeal and mastery of his teachings. If we claim to really know the Lord, we also ought to have the certainty and conviction by faith to trust and obey his Word, no matter how daunting the circumstance appears when called to follow him.

CHAPTER 24

The Futility of Self-Righteousness to Salvation

Jesus himself could not have said any clearer that it is impossible for man to be saved without God (Matthew 19:25–26; Acts 4:12). Attending religious services, doing works of mercy, listening to preaching or sermons are all good, but by itself will not produce salvation of one's soul. It will not close the gap between man and God. Anything that originates from man cannot be the way. Jesus himself said that he is the door to eternal life, he is the only way (John 14:6). It is never about the wretched man reaching out to God, but God reaching out to sinful man who needs to be rescued.

Even the lofty standards of righteousness which the Jewish religious leaders and teachers of law have set in Jesus' time have failed. Jesus says so in Matthew 5:20, "For I tell you, unless your righteousness exceeds that of the scribes and Pharisees, you will never enter the kingdom of heaven." In what way did the learned Scribes and Pharisees missed God's mark?

THE SCRIBES AND PHARISEES

The Pharisees were Jewish members of the largest and most influential religious-political group in the New Testament times. They believed in the resurrection of the dead. They were known

The Futility of Self-Righteousness to Salvation

to be legalistic in following the moral codes and traditions of the fathers—emphasizing strict adherence and compliance to the Old Testament laws without the vital examination of attitude and heart.

They believed that the Law of God given to Moses was twofold:

- Written Moral Laws—etched into the two tablets of the God-given Ten Commandments.

- Oral Ceremonial Laws—consist of the teachings of the prophets and the oral traditions of the Jewish people which today form the practice of Judaism. They strictly observed these religious practices.

The Scribes, on the other hand, were also a large distinct group who had knowledge of the law. They did the job of preserving scripture very seriously, methodically copying, and recopying Old Testament texts with utmost care and correctness. They were also tasked to draft legal documents during their time, such as contracts for marriage, sale of land, and the like. Some Scribes were Pharisees as well.

The folly of self-righteousness was aptly demonstrated by the mindset and life testimonies of many Pharisees and Scribes. Most were outwardly godly and pious, but inwardly sanctimonious and proud. Jesus saw right through their heads and the content of their hearts. They spent long years learning the Old Testament Scriptures. They were aware of the many prophecies concerning the coming Messiah; yet their unbelieving hearts prevented them from recognizing the Savior Jesus when they came face to face with him. They heard Jesus teach, saw him perform signs and wonders, and witnessed how the Lord transformed the lives of people who sought refuge in him. Yet the hearts of many Pharisees and Scribes remained unmoved; their love for God ended with their love to preach and enforce strict compliance of the Old Testament laws.

The inability of the Pharisees to openly receive Jesus stems from a hidden moral decay and corruptness. Their hearts were hardened with pride, envy, self-righteousness, and a legalistic observance of external ceremonial forms. Many of them were offended to see Jesus, with no pedigree training like them, drawing the attention of people because of his wisdom and authority in teaching the laws of God. They could not accept that Jesus, coming from a lowly background, could be the promised Messiah. Since they could not deny the sound teachings and miraculous healings and provisions that Jesus did, they sought to disparage it by attributing Jesus' works as coming from the devil. They had no real love and desire to come to the Holy One of God in the first place, and even actively opposed and plotted to kill him.

During that time in early Israel, the Pharisees and Scribes were the scholarly elite and learned group, highly regarded as authorities in the knowledge and practice of the scriptures and things of God. But how did Jesus see them from the perspective of the kingdom of God? Jesus strongly denounced them as religious hypocrites, calling them out in a series of forceful woes:

> "Woe to you, scribes and Pharisees, hypocrites! For you are like whitewashed tombs, which outwardly appear beautiful, but within are full of dead people's bones and all uncleanness. So you also outwardly appear righteous to others, but within you are full of hypocrisy and lawlessness."
>
> Matthew 23:27–28
>
> "Then Jesus said to the crowds and to his disciples, 'The scribes and the Pharisees sit on Moses' seat, so do and observe whatever they tell you, but not the works they do. For they preach, but do not practice. They tie up heavy burdens, hard to bear, and lay them on people's shoulders, but they themselves are not willing to move them with their finger. They do all their deeds to be seen by others. For they make their phylacteries broad and their fringes long, and they love the place of honor at feasts and the best seats in the synagogues and greetings in the marketplaces and being called rabbi by others.'"
>
> Matthew 23:1–7

In our world today, let us beware of the many Scribes and Pharisees we still encounter in our midst. Let us take heed that we ourselves are not reckoned by others to be like Pharisees or Scribes. We may come across them at work or school or find them hanging around inside our churches. They wear robes of self-righteousness, and their hearts are far from God. Many even know their bible and do not doubt its truth, yet the holy book hardly has an influence over their lifestyle. Their natural inclination is to please man more than God. They are not submitted to Jesus, but rather the *self* is the one in command. They appear to be faithful and religious, but in reality, are ruled by pride and are half-hearted concerning the things of God. They are quick to fight for their own rights, and advocate for the rights of others, but not the right of God to rule over the affairs of man in this world.

In contrast, Jesus counsels those who are looking to become his followers, "The greatest among you shall be your servant. Whoever exalts himself will be humbled, and whoever humbles himself will be exalted" (Matthew 23:11–12).

MENTAL ASSENT AND HEAD KNOWLEDGE

Mere knowledge and belief in Christ will not save the soul. This is no different from the devil who also believes in the one true God and shudders. Says James 2:19 (NKJV), "You believe that there is one God. You do well. Even the demons believe—and tremble!" Multiple accounts in the bible show the authority of Jesus over demons, who were compelled to obey his word every time Jesus commanded them to flee. Satan and the unclean spirits believe that Jesus is the Christ. They know that one day, Jesus will judge the world and throw them down to the fiery place of torment where they belong.

This then begs the question, is God impressed when we profess that we believe in Jesus? Surely not. Believing is not always synonymous with saving faith. Many people believe in God, yet their hearts remain unchanged. Many today attend church and diligently practice their religious duties yet know nothing about the gospel of Christ. We must go further than believing and liking and hearing about Jesus. We must have a clear understanding of who Jesus is and what he has done for us, as proven by the word of God.

Part V: The Folly of Self-Righteousness

Once we properly understand the redemptive work of God based on the revelation of his Word, saving us in the person of his Son, the natural and rightful response ought to be casting ourselves to Jesus and making him our all. The depth of condescension that Jesus went through to reconcile man with God is staggering. God's provision of grace through the incarnate Jesus is unmatched, taking him from the heights of heaven to the pit of hell—all for the sake of us sinners who have forsaken and neglected his love.

Consider these lines from an ode on the grace of Christ by the puritan Thomas Watson, commended to us for reflection in the book *An Ocean of Grace; A Journey to Easter with Great Voices from the Past* by author Tim Chester:

> He took our flesh, that he might give us his Spirit.
>
> He lay in the manger, that we might lie in paradise.
>
> He came down from heaven, that he might bring us to heaven.
>
> And what was all this but love?
>
> Unless our hearts are rocks,
>
> this love of Christ should affect us—
>
> a love that surpasses knowledge![1]

Unless we are gripped with a sense of sin in us, accept in humility that we are lost in sin, and put our faith in the crucified Lord as our Savior, we have no hope. As in the admonition of John the Baptist, the precursor of Christ, repentance and transformation is still the same call being asked of us today. This is hardest for man to do because it offends him to be called a sinner. It is offensive for man to think that he is not worthy, especially those who do many wonderful, exemplary works. Many good people stumble to receive the Lord's gospel because it demands man to see himself the way God sees him—blinded by sin and in need of a Savior. Christianity is difficult because it requires humility and submission to the authority of Jesus. It requires courage and conviction to call sin as sin. It requires choosing the hard, often lonely path to following Christ,

---

1. Chester, *An Ocean of Grace*, 129.

The Futility of Self-Righteousness to Salvation

against the easy, popular, pleasurable choice of conforming to the world. Real Christianity demands holiness in all areas big and small of our daily practical life.

As final illustration, let's look at the biblical account of the self-righteous scribe in Mark 12:28–34. The scribe asked Jesus which command was the most important of all. In response, Jesus summed up the Ten Commandments given by God to Moses into the most important command (v30–31): "And you shall love the Lord your God with all your heart and with all your soul and with all your mind and with all your strength. The second is this: You shall love your neighbor as yourself. There is no other commandment greater than these." Acknowledging the answer of Jesus as right, the scribe took it a notch higher by saying that to love God with all your heart, understanding, and strength, and to love your neighbor as yourself, is far more important than all the burnt offerings and sacrifices.

Jesus affirmed the scribe's sensible answer and told him (v34), "You are not far from the kingdom of God." Not far? What exactly did Jesus mean saying the scribe is almost in the kingdom, but not quite there yet? Jesus saw that the scribe had a good grasp of biblical teachings; however, it is still just head knowledge and mental assent. Mere knowledge of God's teachings is not enough to open the gate of God's kingdom for the scribe to enter. He was close to the kingdom but not there yet. The scribe needed a "change of heart" procedure that can only be done by the Lord himself. Entry to heaven depends not on the state of man's head but on the state of his heart.

When the gospel is preached to people who consider themselves to be upright or good, many do not really listen because they believe they know it already. Many think that the good news of the gospel is for the obvious sinners only, the notorious offenders in society who commit the observable sins. Take for example the many good, prayerful people who say they believe and trust in Jesus, yet on the next breath, they constantly worry about this and that. Worries and anxieties over things in life take our eyes away from the Lord. Worry emanates from a spirit of pride. Why? Because it puts the worrying person in a posture where he thinks he can take control and do the action needed to resolve things. Ironically, most of the time he could not, because man has no absolute control over everything. In truth, worry demonstrates faith in ourselves and lack of faith in God. Letting go of worries and anxieties is hard because it requires humility (1 Peter 5:6–7). It bruises our sense of self to face up and accept that there is little we can do to fix or remedy certain things in life.

On the other hand, there are professing believers who practice crisis faith, meaning they only run to Jesus when they are in trouble, when their backs are against the wall and there's no way out. As last recourse, they remember to pray to God and ask him to take them out of their predicament. When God answers their prayers, they are grateful for sure; but after a while, they typically forget about God and return to the world which they love, unconverted and unchanged.

Many are invited or called but few are chosen (Matthew 22:14). Entry to God's kingdom is not a matter of intellectual pursuit and head knowledge; it is not gained with outward forms of godliness or with a passport of self-righteousness. As Jesus said in Matthew 7:21–23 (NKJV), "Not everyone who says to Me, 'Lord, Lord,' shall enter the kingdom of heaven, but he who does the will of My Father in heaven. Many will say to me in that day, 'Lord, Lord, have we not prophesied in your name, cast out demons in your name, and done many wonders in your name?' And then I will declare to them, 'I never knew you; depart from me, you who practice lawlessness!'"

True conversion to God is hard to come by. Few are inclined to be gripped by sin; few are moved by a compelling need for Christ. This is impossible for man to do, unless God provides the grace and means for it. As many preachers teach, even the devil can say that Christ is *a savior*; but only a redeemed soul can say that Christ is *my Savior and Lord*. Faith in Jesus pleases God. Mere knowledge of God that is not accompanied by faith does not impress him.

Only with true repentance and faith in Jesus are we made acceptable to God the Father. Scripture says that you shall bear fruit when you let Jesus rule over your life and heart (John 15:4–5). This means that you set aside your own will and obey the purpose and will of Jesus for your life. This is how salvation through Christ results in good works.

The Futility of Self-Righteousness to Salvation

Continuing to see ourselves as good people is almost like telling Jesus, *It's okay, Lord, I've got this. Thank you but don't worry about me. I can figure things out by myself.* Many who see themselves as worthy, righteous, and lacking nothing have wittingly or unwittingly slammed the door on Jesus' face, so to speak. But gracious as he always is, Jesus does not push himself to those who do not have a sincere need for him. Jesus longs to be wanted. Shunned by the self-sufficient ones, Jesus calls to himself the weary and the heavy-laden, those who carry in them a load from which they could not set themselves free—the load of rejection, unforgiveness, shame, or worry. Jesus says in Luke 5:32 (NKJV), "I have not come to call the righteous, but sinners, to repentance." No matter how much progress we think we make in our walk with God, we have not made any progress at all unless we realize our need for Jesus to be our Lord.

But what does it look like to submit and give Jesus authority over our life? It entails first a genuine desire to know the Lord. It is impossible for us to love or submit to somebody whom we do not know. Do we know God as he has revealed himself savingly in the person of his son Jesus? Remember that knowledge of God has little or nothing to do with religion; a person can be religious but not have knowledge of God. During this end-time period, God has appointed the means to know him through his Word, through his church (people of God), and through the work of the Holy Spirit. We will talk about this more in the next part of this book.

Submitting to Jesus means honoring and obeying his Word, whether in secret or out in the open. It means putting Jesus first, placing our trust and dependence on him—even if doing so does not make sense to the people around us and the world is doing the contrary.

In other words, giving Jesus authority over our life is not easy; in fact, it can be very, very difficult. It will cost us something. It will require us to hand over control—which is particularly tough for many good, hardworking, self-reliant people.

Heeding the call to become a follower of Christ is not for the faint-hearted.

As author John Snyder says in his devotional study, "Behold Your God: The Weight of Majesty":

Part V: The Folly of Self-Righteousness

"Christian progress is not up; it's down. We are growing in humility. We are becoming more aware of how needy we've always been, and more aware of how sufficient Christ really is. And so there's this wonderful expanse that's growing in our minds. I am much needier than I ever imagined and He is infinitely full for people like me."[2]

---

2. Snyder, "Behold Your God: The Weight of Majesty."

PART VI

What Must Good People Do to Have Eternal Life

CHAPTER 25

The Consequence of Man's Fall

The book of Genesis in the bible reveals God's original plan for creating a perfect place, where his kingdom is established, where he rules as fatherly king over a people whom he created to love, protect, and bless. The God of the heavens and the earth is all-sufficient. He lacks nothing nor does he need anything, but out of his good pleasure, God made man according to his image to enjoy his presence and his blessing. The Almighty God purposed man to ascribe glory to him by endowing man with physical and mental faculties, entrusting to him all the wondrous natural creation God had made. He gave man the responsibility to rule and have dominion over the earth as stated in Genesis 1—2. God intended man to thrive, enjoy, and walk alongside him in fellowship forever.

THE FALL OF MAN

God placed Adam and Eve in the Garden of Eden to tend and keep it. The Lord God filled the garden with all kinds of generous provisions for Adam and Eve to live on, work on, and enjoy. God made all kinds of trees that grow luscious leaves and fruits, good for food. God blessed them with abundance and fullness of life. But God also gave them instruction not to eat from the tree of the knowledge of good and evil. This tree marks God's sovereignty and authority above all. God alone is the creator; and all created beings, including man, are subject to his rule.

God made this truth clear to Adam and Eve for distinct reasons. Firstly, God cannot deny who he is. He is supremely eminent; there is nothing and no one above him. God is the source of all life and things; he owns and presides over everything. Secondly, God commands obedience from man not for his own sake, but for man's highest good. Let us not miss in this the loving and protective fatherly heart of God. He wanted man to understand that life, happiness, and rest are found only in unity with God; outside of God, there is only death, emptiness, and toil. God spoke to Adam and Eve with clarity and cautioned them not to eat from the forbidden tree, or else they will die and be separated from him. How immensely kind God is to extend such grace, protectively counseling Adam and Eve as if to say, *I love you and I want to bless you. Abide in me, listen to me, be my people. Demonstrate your love to me by obeying what I say.*

Alas, Adam and Eve disobeyed, and committed the one thing God forbade them to do. They chose to believe Satan's lies, in place of God's word. They showed contempt over what God had richly bestowed upon them and coveted what God did not see fit to give them. Instead of trusting God, Adam and Eve decided to rely on themselves to determine what is right and wrong. They were captivated by the idea to be like God, as the devil tempted them to believe, exposing a heart attitude that portends pride and rebellion against God. They willfully fell into sin, bringing the world down with them, spoiling everything good that God intended for all creation. Sin tarnished and broke the relationship between man and the holy God; in the same way that sin caused brokenness over relationships among men themselves.

DEATH, THE CURSE OF SIN

It was not part of God's design for man to experience death. But because of sin, man was cursed with a sinful nature and became subject to three types of death—physical, spiritual, and eternal death.

The Consequence of Man's Fall

The decline of man's body and the eventual separation of his body from soul, returning to dust from which he was made—this is physical death. In physical death, man's body was cursed and subjected to hard work, weakness, infirmities, afflictions, and decay.

The separation of man's soul and spirit from the presence of God—this is spiritual death. The spirit of man is his connection to the Spirit of God. With the curse of sin, the communication line between God and man is severed. Apart from God, man could be physically alive, but he is spiritually dead.

By nature, the fallen man is subject to God's wrath at the end of days. As Ephesians 2:3 aptly describes, "—among whom we all once lived in the passions of our flesh, carrying out the desires of the body and the mind, and were by nature children of wrath, like the rest of mankind." Our fallen body and soul need to be redeemed. Without redemption, man's body and soul shall be forever separated from God—which is eternal death.

The bible categorically states that man will experience physical death once and after that the judgment of God (Hebrews 9:27). After physical death, the unsaved souls who rejected Christ are immediately cast into Sheol (Hebrew word in Old Testament) or Hades (Greek word in New Testament), an interim abode of agony and anguish. Sheol or Hades is a hostile place of absolute darkness, bleakness, and torment—a place cut off from God and his light and love. Whether we accept it or not, death is real and there will surely be a separation—where the redeemed will be united with Christ in rest and joy, and the unredeemed cast off to eternal torment and misery in hades or hell.

Jesus himself alluded to the truth about this physical separation between those who are his and those who are not:

> "So it was that the beggar died and was carried away by the angels to Abraham's bosom. The rich man also died and was buried. And being in torments in Hades, he lifted up his eyes and saw Abraham afar off, and Lazarus in his bosom. Then he cried and said, 'Father Abraham, have mercy on me, and send Lazarus that he may dip the tip of his finger in water and cool my tongue; for I am tormented in this flame.' But Abraham said, 'Son,

remember that in your lifetime you received your good things, and likewise Lazarus evil things; but now he is comforted and you are tormented. And besides all this, between us and you there is a great gulf fixed, so that those who want to pass from here to you cannot, nor can those from there pass to us."

Luke 16:22-26 (NKJV)

Sin placed man under the condemnation and wrath of the holy God. We have belabored this point in the previous chapters, learning the biblical truth why it is not possible for God to co-exist with sin. God is relentlessly opposed to sin because of his holy and pure nature. As one crack on an ice sheet exposes it to fracture and break into pieces, so does one sin poisons the soul and strikes against the holiness of God. By choosing to sin, man risked losing communion with God and relinquished the blessing of his presence. More than physical death and spiritual death, let us fear most and do our uttermost to escape eternal death—where both man's body and soul shall be separated from God forevermore.

UNDERSTANDING THE SINFUL NATURE OF MAN

When man sinned, God acted accordingly. And always, the Lord Almighty's actions remain true to his nature as the God of justice, mercy, and love (Genesis 3:14-19, NKJV).

To the woman Eve, the Lord God said (v16), "I will greatly multiply your sorrow and your conception; In pain you shall bring forth children; Your desire shall be for your husband, And he shall rule over you."

To the man Adam, the Lord God said (v17-19), "Cursed is the ground for your sake; In toil you shall eat of it all the days of your life. Both thorns and thistles it shall bring forth for you, and you shall eat the herb of the field. In the sweat of your face you shall eat bread till you return to the ground, For out of it you were taken; For dust you are, and to dust you shall return."

The Lord God made tunics of animal skin and clothed Adam and Eve. God banished them out of the Garden of Eden, lest they

The Consequence of Man's Fall

eat of the tree of life and live forever in their sinful state. Sin drove man away from the presence of God and placed man outside of fellowship with him, otherwise known as spiritual death.

Outside of God, Adam and Eve and all generations after them until today are caught in total depravity of sin. Every person descended from Adam is by nature born into the cursed and wretched condition of sin. This truth on man's sinful nature is clearly and repeatedly established in the word of God. Here are a few supporting scripture verses from the Old Testament and New Testament books:

> "Therefore, just as sin came into the world through one man, and death through sin, and so death spread to all men because all sinned—"
>
> Romans 5:12
>
> "The fool says in his heart, 'There is no God.' They are corrupt, they do abominable deeds; there is none who does good. The Lord looks down from heaven on the children of man, to see if there are any who understand, who seek after God. They have all turned aside; together they have become corrupt; there is none who does good, not even one."
>
> Psalm 14:1–3
>
> "Surely there is not a righteous man on earth who does good and never sins."
>
> Ecclesiastes 7:20
>
> "If we say we have no sin, we deceive ourselves, and the truth is not in us. If we confess our sins, he is faithful and just to forgive us our sins and to cleanse us from all unrighteousness. If we say we have not sinned, we make him a liar, and his word is not in us."
>
> 1 John 1:8–10

It is critical that we get a clear and correct understanding of what the word of God means when it says that man by nature is sinful. Pastor Nathan Sawyer reiterated this spot-on point made by the

Part VI: What Must Good People Do to Have Eternal Life

Rev. Gilbert Tennent in his historic sermon "Total Depravity—The Wretched State of the Unconverted":

> "The God of truth declares that the natural man is not sick or weak as some tell us, but dead. Hence conversion is said to be a quickening or resurrection from the dead."[1]

Tennent, a seventeenth century Great Awakening revivalist and preacher, went on to teach that man, left to himself, is devoid of all spiritual good, ignorant of all spiritual good, and impotent or unable to do any good.

The tyrannical power of sin dominates the nature of man from birth, rendering corrupt all his ways, thoughts, desires. Psalm 51:5 alludes to this when it says, "Behold, I was brought forth in iniquity, and in sin did my mother conceive me." It is not merely that our behavior is wrong or what we do is wrong, but sinful is who we are. From birth, we are tainted with sin, because we had inherited a sinful nature way back from our original parents Adam and Eve. Unfortunately, the bible teaches that apart from the redeeming grace of God, there is nothing we can do to change this condition. "And you were dead in the trespasses and sins in which you once walked, following the course of this world, following the prince of the power of the air, the spirit that is now at work in the sons of disobedience—" (Ephesians 2:1–2).

Sin has rendered us ignorant and slow in understanding the things of God. Without the work of the Godhead Father, Son, and Spirit, convicting us and drawing us to repentance and faith, there is nothing in us that will make us seek and follow God. Says 1 Corinthians 2:14, "The natural person does not accept the things of the Spirit of God, for they are folly to him, and he is not able to understand them because they are spiritually discerned." Our flesh is naturally drawn to the cares, pleasures, and pursuits of the world. We do not have a natural appetite for things concerning God. By nature, our mind is closed and our will opposed to God.

Sans the renewing and transforming work of the Holy Spirit in us, consider how difficult it is to sit still and read and understand the

---

1. Sawyer, "A Re-Preaching of the Historic Sermon by Gilbert Tennent."

The Consequence of Man's Fall

word of God. Many today consider it foolishness, a waste of time, even fanatical to sing in private worship unto God, and to camp in our closet for sustained prayer and fellowship with Jesus. We naturally crave for the praise of man and think less about offending God. As written in Jeremiah 17:9, "The heart is deceitful above all things, and desperately sick; who can understand it?" We forget that the things that matter most to God are not the ones that we do on the outside, but rather the ones that come from within our heart.

Lest we conclude that we are less guilty since we have no control over our sinful nature that makes us unable to follow after God, know that depravity has also made us unwilling to come to God on his terms. By nature, we resist to know God for who he is, to surrender our will for his, and to abide with him by faith. "And without faith it is impossible to please him, for whoever would draw near to God must believe that he exists and that he rewards those who seek him" (Hebrews 11:6).

We customarily offer God things that we think pleases him, things that our religion teaches us to do, without care about examining the content of our heart. Religion has a way to paint a picture of God that is imagined by man, not the God of the bible. Religion without regeneration promotes a presumption of faith and a dependence on good works, which are stumbling blocks to saving faith. For the Lord considers it foolishness to attach importance to the cleansing of the body when the cleansing of the heart is overlooked (Luke 11:39). We see this clearly in the plight of the Pharisees, many of whom Jesus called out as religious hypocrites. External devoutness, bowed head, raised hands become unacceptable to God when the heart is not changed, grieved, or moved to repentance by sin. The idea that man can be devout before they are transformed by grace, repentance, and faith in the Lord Jesus is a subtle and clever manipulation by the devil.

We must learn to discern very carefully between doing good works and depending upon it for the salvation of our soul. Here again is part of Rev. Gilbert Tennent's forceful but biblically astute discourse on the danger and fallacy of trusting and relying on external good works to become approved of God. To quote from his sermon "Total Depravity—The Wretched State of the Unconverted":

Part VI: What Must Good People Do to Have Eternal Life

> "Those that believe should be careful to maintain good works, for they are good and profitable unto men. But works done before faith and justification are not good, properly speaking. And it is such I have been discoursing. Works may be of manifold use, though they do not justify. Gold is good, though it cannot be eaten. I do not discourage from doing good works, but only from depending upon them. Such dependence is fatal to the souls of men. We should labor as though we could be justified by works, yet depend no more upon them than if we did nothing."[2]

Good works cannot produce salvation, but rather they are the result and evidence of salvation. As Ephesians 2:10 states, "For we are his workmanship, created in Christ Jesus for good works, which God prepared beforehand, that we should walk in them." Jesus came not only to rescue us but to make us good, to make us do good works. Realize that even our good works are a gift from God; therefore, we ought not to take merit or distinction in them. How truly noble and wise are the ways of God from the ways of men. What a profoundly good and amazing God we have!

---

2. Sawyer, "A Re-Preaching of the Historic Sermon by Gilbert Tennent."

CHAPTER 26

The Compassion of God for the Lost

Now having understood the biblical truth that goodness does not dwell in our natural sinful state, what are we to do? Where do we hide when God is our enemy, and we are headed for the wrath of God? Even if we desire to do what is right, we are impotent to carry it out, "For I know that nothing good dwells in me, that is, in my flesh. For I have the desire to do what is right, but not the ability to carry it out" (Romans 7:18). Who can deliver us from this cursed and miserable state?

The startling answer is it is God himself in the person of his Son who can rescue man from the bondage of sin. Alongside the warning of judgment and wrath by a just God who demands that sin be punished, God extends an invitation for man to take refuge in his loving and holy provisions.

We see this in the first act of love that God showed Adam and Eve when they fell into sin—he covered with sheep skin the nakedness and shame caused by their disobedience. This act required a shedding of the blood of a slain animal, out of which the animal skin covering was made to clothe Adam and Eve. This was the first recorded redemptive manifestation of God's mercy and grace to sinful man. Though Adam and Eve were punished with physical and spiritual death for their sins, God showed mercy to them with the provision of the animal skin covering to replace the man-made leaf clothing that they made. Banished from the garden, Adam and Eve left God's presence clothed in God's kindness and compassion.

We also see God's provision in the Old Testament sacrificial offering and cleansing, which God instituted as temporary means for his chosen people to atone for their sins. The Old Testament Israelites repeatedly gathered for the ceremonial killing and shedding of blood of unblemished animals such as goats and sheep, for the forgiveness of sins of both the officiating priest and the Jewish congregation.

We also see God's great love time and again, when he sent prophets after prophets to warn his people Israel against impending calamities, attacks, and captivity by strong evil armies; lest they do not repent from their idolatry and return to God. As documented in biblical historical accounts, many of these prophetic messengers were persecuted, ignored, or killed by Israel who refused to believe and heed the warnings God gave again and again through the prophets.

Taking all this into account, the immense love of the faithful Almighty God never wavered. The pattern of early provisions foreshadowed the ultimate perfect and complete sacrifice of God's own son Jesus Christ on the cross. In God's appointed time, he sent not just another human prophet but his divine heir, Jesus the Messiah, to reconcile sinful man back to himself. God has condescended to embrace the dust from which mankind was made by appointing his own son to become man and be the mediator for man's sin. Although death is the punishment for sinners, God clearly does not want men to perish without hope, and that hope is placed in the person of the Lord Jesus alone.

While God is a God of justice, he also is a God of love who offers forgiveness and restoration. So how does God's love serve the rightful demand of justice to punish sinful human beings, but at the same time save them from spiritual and eternal death? How does God grant eternal life to a lost soul?

God's love for man established the covenant of grace in the seed of a woman, Christ the Messiah, to restore man from the spiritual death caused by sin. God prophesied the ultimate defeat of Satan through Jesus, the spoken seed. "And she will bring forth a

The Compassion of God for the Lost

Son, and you shall call His name Jesus, for He will save His people from their sins" (Matthew 1:21, NKJV).

The God of justice, love, and mercy provided a way out of the doom, which the rebellious, sinful men brought upon themselves. God's appointed way is through the shedding of the blood, by substitution, by imputed righteousness, by faith, through repentance and forgiveness, by God's grace alone. It is not by human efforts, good works, man-made morality, and religious exercises that a sinner can be reconciled to God. There is nothing in us or in what we do that can save us from eternal damnation. Instead, there is everything in Jesus the Servant-Savior, who lived without sin and who died sacrificially as our sin-bearer on the cross, that is most acceptable and pleasing to God the Father. Jesus bore all the punishment due our sins. His sacrifice and finished work on the cross fully satisfied the justice that God demanded as recompense for our sin.

> "For our sake he made him to be sin who knew no sin, so that in him we might become the righteousness of God."
>
> 2 Corinthians 5:21

CHAPTER 27

Jesus, the Only Way

Jesus voluntarily came to earth as a man, knowing that he was to die on the cross to atone for sin and reconcile man to God. Shortly before Jesus' departure for Calvary, this conversation with his disciples was recorded in the book of John:

> "'And if I go and prepare a place for you, I will come again and will take you to myself, that where I am you may be also. And you know the way to where I am going.' Thomas said to him, 'Lord, we do not know where you are going. How can we know the way?' Jesus said to him, 'I am the way, and the truth, and the life. No one comes to the Father except through me.'"
>
> John 14:3–6

The pursuing love of God has covenanted the way for man to be restored back to him through Jesus. This covenant is only by Jesus Christ and only to those who believe in him, "For God so loved the world that He gave His only begotten Son, that whoever believes in Him should not perish but have everlasting life" (John 3:16, NKJV).

Believing means placing our trust and faith, not on ourselves but in Jesus, in his words, and in what he has accomplished for us at the cross. We need to realize that Jesus knowingly went through the tortuous suffering, shame, and death on the cross—because of his love for sinful, impenitent man. Scripture says no greater love can compare to what Jesus did, that he lay down his life for his friends

(John 15:13). If we are to become friends with Jesus, we have got to personally receive and embrace what he did for us at the cross. Nobody else in the world, no other faith or spiritual leader in the world, can offer this kind of friendship. This is the same covenantal relationship that the people of Israel made with God in Nehemiah 9 when they humbled themselves before God, recounted the many mercies of God, cried in repentance before God, and confessed their sins. After which says Nehemiah 9:38, "Because of all this we make a firm covenant in writing; on the sealed document are the names of our princes, our Levites, and our priests."

Individually, when we make the decision to take God's free offer of grace and forgiveness through Jesus, we enter into a covenant or union in faith with Jesus. We need not memorialize this union in writing as Nehemiah and the Israelites did, but a truly renewed person in Christ shall be marked by a changed heart, changed lifestyle, and changed valuations in life. We start to live our everyday life with the mindfulness that we are not our own, but that we belong to God. As the apostle Paul writes in 2 Corinthians 5:16–17, "From now on, therefore, we regard no one according to the flesh. Even though we once regarded Christ according to the flesh, we regard him thus no longer. Therefore, if anyone is in Christ, he is a new creation. The old has passed away; behold, the new has come." The blood of Jesus through his atoning death on the cross confers on us this newness of life; from being spiritually dead in sin, we become reborn in the resurrection life of Jesus (John 3:3–5).

Here we must make an important distinction. The answer to the question *What does a man do in order to be saved?* is different from the answer to the question *What does a saved man do?*

In the first question *What does a man do in order to be saved?*— there is nothing a man can do to be saved except to be convinced of his utter sinfulness. This Spirit-led conviction compels man to ask God for forgiveness, believe, and take refuge in Jesus whom God provisioned as recompense for sin. It is an act of the soul, an act of the will. It is an informed decision that we make after we hear the God-revealed gospel of Jesus Christ and believe in it.

When we do, God promises to set us free from the cursed and wretched condition we adopted by nature. It is the grace of God

Part VI: What Must Good People Do to Have Eternal Life

through our faith in the finished work of Jesus that delivers us from all wickedness caused by sin. We cannot earn our way to heaven. It is not by merit, good behavior, or works of mercy that we get saved. As we said before, the magnitude of our sin cannot be covered by any works or service we do. It is God who ordains the acceptable way back to him. God did not ask man to do good deeds to be saved from sin. Ephesians 2:9 says it is "not a result of works, so that no one may boast." Out of his abundant love and kindness, God chose his son Jesus to do the high priestly work of redeeming man from sin (Hebrews 5:4–10). Salvation to eternal life is not something that is done by us or through us; it is something that Jesus did for us.

> "But when the goodness and loving kindness of God our Savior appeared, he saved us, not because of works done by us in righteousness, but according to his own mercy, by the washing of regeneration and renewal of the Holy Spirit, whom he poured out on us richly through Jesus Christ our Savior, so that being justified by his grace we might become heirs according to the hope of eternal life."
>
> Titus 3:4–7

Once we resolve to put our faith in Christ as our Lord, the bible says that we are justified or made right in the sight of God, we are adopted into the family of God, and we have been positioned to now belong to Christ. This is what the verse above alludes to when it says we "become heirs according to the hope of eternal life" (v7).

In the second question *What does a saved man do?*— this points to how we live out in practice the new identity we inherited in Christ. Though we have already been forgiven and accepted in Christ, note that we still live in a sinful world, and we still inhabit our sinful bodies. As such, we must overcome and put to death the areas in our life that come against our identity of belonging to Jesus. The bible refers to this as the process of sanctification, when we are to live differently from the world, set apart and made holy for God, just as Jesus is holy.

> "But you were washed, you were sanctified, you were justified in the name of the Lord Jesus Christ and by the Spirit of our God."
>
> 1 Corinthians 6:11

Jesus, the Only Way

Just as we did not earn our justification, so too we cannot achieve our sanctification without the grace of God. The Lord promised and gave the assurance that he who follows him will never walk in darkness but in light (John 8:12). "Draw near to God, and he will draw near to you," says James 4:8. Jesus will not leave in ignorance those who come to depend by faith in him; he promised to provide instruction and help. A man who receives Jesus as his Lord need not waver in uncertainty or doubt; there is security in Christ once we belong to him.

Ephesians 1:13–14 gives us this guarantee that God will complete the work of salvation that he started in our life, "In him you also, when you heard the word of truth, the gospel of your salvation, and believed in him, were sealed with the promised Holy Spirit, who is the guarantee of our inheritance until we acquire possession of it, to the praise of his glory."

Man can count on God's Counselor (the Holy Spirit), God's word, and God's people to walk alongside him on his way to heaven. Jesus may not be here today in bodily form, but he discloses his power and his presence in and through us by means of his Spirit, his Word, and the church body of Christ. All these provisions are available to each of us now, and it is to the great benefit of our soul if we seek and engage in it.

The fruit of a saved man's life is marked by humility, persevering prayers, a lifestyle of worship/gratefulness to God, bible reading and meditation, and kindness to others in word and deed. One can only bear this fruit with the enabling grace of God. The chief means of grace that the Lord provisioned for us at this time is through the power of the Holy Spirit, the instructive word of God, and the prayers and encouragement of brothers and sisters in Christ. Faith does not insulate us from the difficulties in life. Jesus did not say that walking with him is easy, but he promised that we shall not walk alone. Those who take refuge in Christ are not left at the mercy of chance, but are sustained by the eternal arms of God, the fullness of his strength and saving power underneath (Deuteronomy 33:27).

Once we commit to the decision to live under Christ's rule, the word of God says that the heavenly Father begins to see us differently; we become acceptable in his eyes. How is this so? How can it be that when we repent from our sins, trust in Christ, and make him our Lord, we become justified in the sight of God? What does Romans 8:1 (NKJV) mean when it says, "There is therefore now no condemnation to those who are in Christ Jesus, who do not walk according to the flesh, but according to the Spirit."

Let us look into the basic biblical truths behind the triune God's redemptive work by grace. Remember, the restorative work for the removal of sin was procured by the incarnate son Jesus Christ on the cross. Christ "became the source of eternal salvation" (Hebrews 5:9) to those who receive and obey him.

BY THE BLOOD OF JESUS

In the first Passover, God's people escaped judgment by applying the blood of the sacrificial lamb on their doorposts. The destroyer passed over every house protected by the blood. In the same way, we are protected by the blood that Jesus shed on the cross. Jesus is the Passover lamb that saves our lives from bondage to sin and death.

The Old Testament prophetic act of killing unblemished animals to offer to God as atonement for sin, pointed to the real blood sacrifice of God's only son Jesus Christ. It is only through the shed blood of Jesus, with his suffering and death on the cross, that man can be saved. Without Jesus dying and shedding his blood on the cross, we will never have forgiveness and remission of our sins.

> "And if you call on him as Father who judges impartially according to each one's deeds, conduct yourselves with fear throughout the time of your exile, knowing that you were ransomed from the futile ways inherited from your forefathers, not with perishable things such as silver or gold, but with the precious blood of Christ, like that of a lamb without blemish or spot."
>
> 1 Peter 1:17–19

Jesus, the Only Way

BY SUBSTITUTION ON THE CROSS

Jesus took the curse for all our sins, including all sicknesses, diseases, and the death sentence for our sinfulness (Galatians 3:13). He bore them all in his broken body and shed blood as a sacrificial act of redemption. He willingly offered his life to die in our stead. Jesus did not bleed and suffer because he was vanquished or overpowered by his enemies. Jesus laid his life down of his own accord because he loved us (John 10:18). In the eyes of God, Jesus Christ became the sinner who deserved the punishment of death. Jesus who knew no sin became sin for us. He took the punishment that we deserve and experienced hell so that we may escape it.

Jesus left the glory of heaven and became man as the substitute or atonement for our sins. How can we be sure of this?—because Jesus himself said so. In John 12:27–28, we hear the Man-God Jesus groan at his impending death on the cross, troubled by the horrific pain and suffering he will go through as the full weight of our sin is imputed on him, "'Now is my soul troubled. And what shall I say? "Father, save me from this hour"? But for this purpose I have come to this hour. Father, glorify your name.' Then a voice came from heaven: 'I have glorified it, and I will glorify it again.'" There is security in Christ because he bore the wrath of God in place of every sinner who takes refuge in him. When the Lord forgives a man, he removes the penalty of wrath caused by sin in man. The Lord Jesus stands in between sin and the curse.

> "And you, being dead in your trespasses and the uncircumcision of your flesh, He has made alive together with Him, having forgiven you all trespasses, having wiped out the handwriting of requirements that was against us, which was contrary to us. And He has taken it out of the way, having nailed it to the cross."
>
> Colossians 2:13–14 (NKJV)

Part VI: What Must Good People Do to Have Eternal Life

BY GRACE THROUGH FAITH

Ephesians 2:8–9 (NKJV) states, "For by grace you have been saved through faith, and that not of yourselves; it is the gift of God, not of works, lest anyone should boast."

The apostle Thomas found it hard to believe when the other disciples told him that they saw the resurrected Lord. Thomas said that if he didn't see the mark of the nails in Jesus, and put his hand into his side, he will never believe. When Thomas came face to face with the resurrected Christ, he taught him a lesson on faith, "Then he said to Thomas, 'Put your finger here, and see my hands; and put out your hand, and place it in my side. Do not disbelieve, but believe.' Thomas answered him, 'My Lord and my God!' Jesus said to him, 'Have you believed because you have seen me? Blessed are those who have not seen and yet have believed'" (John 20:27–29).

The word of God defines faith in Hebrews 11:1–2 (NKJV), "Now faith is the substance of things hoped for, the evidence of things not seen. For by it the elders obtained a good testimony." The faith described here involves a firm conviction and belief in the gospel, in the resurrected Christ, and in the God-assured future reality that is yet unseen. Scripture says that this kind of faith, founded on divine assurance and not on observable evidence, is possible only by God's grace "And this is not your own doing; it is the gift of God" (Ephesians 2:8).

At the core is the object of our faith—the Lord Jesus Christ. Hence it is said that it's not mainly a question of whether one's faith is big or small. What counts is the object of our faith; in whom do we place our trust and belief? If we sincerely receive Christ and seek refuge in him, we become covered under the shadow of divine favor. When God looks at us, he beholds the face of his beloved righteous son Jesus. This is one tenable explanation why God sees us as if we have never sinned, why God sees a sinner like us without spot or wrinkle.

BY REPENTANCE AND CONFESSION

Salvation is by faith. Make no mistake, it is not faith in faith, but faith in what, in whom? Salvation is anchored on faith in the person and the work of Jesus Christ with his death on the cross, and resurrection from death to life. Genuine faith though is not just a mental assent of believing in Christ. Satan knows and acknowledges Jesus as God, but he is hell-bound. Many people in the world believe in Jesus, but he is not the center of their lives. Many go to church, but do not go to Christ. True faith is conditioned upon a sincere awareness and turning away from sin, honest dependence or reliance upon Christ, and a commitment to follow him whatever the cost. Real saving faith must be evident in a regenerated life of holiness with good works as fruit, with a sustained persevering attitude and will of being submitted in all areas of our life to Jesus.

Jesus himself went about preaching the gospel of the kingdom of God to the early believers, calling people to repent and turn away from the sinful ways of the world. Jesus said in Luke 5:32 (NKJV), "I have not come to call the righteous, but sinners, to repentance." True repentance begins with the sense and conviction of one's own sinfulness. If Isaiah, the prophet of God, was so convicted when touched by the presence of the Lord, how much more should we? "And I said: 'Woe is me! For I am lost; for I am a man of unclean lips, and I dwell in the midst of a people of unclean lips; for my eyes have seen the King, the Lord of hosts!'" (Isaiah 6:5).

A repentant sinner is being transformed and sanctified when he begins to hate sin which the heavenly Father hates and takes interest on things in which the Father delights. A repentant sinner becomes acceptable to God only when the Father sees his rebellious heart humbled and clothed with the righteousness of Jesus.

BY IMPUTED RIGHTEOUSNESS

Jesus Christ lived his earthly life without sin; he always upheld righteousness and overcame all temptations of the evil one. He prayed often to God the Father. He was zealous to do God's will and glorify him. But God, in his sovereign wisdom, allowed Christ to suffer and become sin for us. As a result, our loving God imputes or credits the beauty, obedience, and righteousness of Christ to those who admit their sinfulness, accept the work of Christ, and put their faith in him. It is only on account of the strength of Christ's righteousness and the saving work that he accomplished on the cross, that God can accept a repentant sinner.

Let it be known very clearly that there is no good thing in us that can win us God's favor. It is Christ's robe of righteousness upon us which God sees, not our own righteousness. This righteousness is made visible in the actions, choices, and lifestyle of a changed man, who is seriously convinced of the need to belong to Christ, and genuinely transformed by the work of the Holy Spirit. As the prophet Isaiah puts it (Isaiah 51:1), "Listen to me, you who pursue righteousness, you who seek the Lord: look to the rock from which you were hewn, and to the quarry from which you were dug."

> "Indeed, I count everything as loss because of the surpassing worth of knowing Christ Jesus my Lord. For his sake I have suffered the loss of all things and count them as rubbish, in order that I may gain Christ and be found in him, not having a righteousness of my own that comes from the law, but that which comes through faith in Christ, the righteousness from God that depends on faith—"
>
> Philippians 3:8–9

CHAPTER 28

The Path Toward God's Kingdom

Scripture presents the path to eternal life with God the Father through Jesus Christ as follows:

- Acknowledge that God is holy and you are unholy; that you are unrighteous and ungodly, deserving of death and hell; that there is nothing in you that qualifies you to stand before a holy God and become reconciled to him.

    "But nothing unclean will ever enter it, nor anyone who does what is detestable or false, but only those who are written in the Lamb's book of life."

    Revelation 21:27

- Acknowledge that your self-righteousness is as a filthy rag in the eyes of a holy God; that there is nothing good in you, nothing you can do to earn God's salvation for your lost soul.

    "But we are all like an unclean thing,
    And all our righteousnesses are like filthy rags;
    We all fade as a leaf,
    And our iniquities, like the wind,
    Have taken us away."

    Isaiah 64:6 (NKJV)

- Acknowledge that there is a righteousness outside your own self; that righteousness comes from Jesus who lived as a man but sinned not.

   > "And because of him you are in Christ Jesus, who became to us wisdom from God, righteousness and sanctification and redemption,—"
   >
   > 1 Corinthians 1:30

   > "And there is salvation in no one else, for there is no other name under heaven given among men by which we must be saved."
   >
   > Acts 4:12

   > "Although he was a son, he learned obedience through what he suffered. And being made perfect, he became the source of eternal salvation to all who obey him, being designated by God a high priest after the order of Melchizedek."
   >
   > Hebrews 5:8–10

- Acknowledge and realize that the righteousness of Jesus is offered to you freely by faith through God's grace and mercy; that the righteousness of Jesus is credited or imputed upon you as you repent, believe, and submit in faith to Jesus as your Lord and Savior. As you do this, the penalty of being spiritually separated from God because of your sin nature is taken away. Your iniquities and transgressions are forgiven and atoned for, washed clean by the blood of Jesus, and you are clothed with his righteousness. And the Holy Spirit will be available to guide and teach you, to become more like Jesus in words and deeds, as you start your new life in submission to him.

   > "For our sake he made him to be sin who knew no sin, so that in him we might become the righteousness of God."
   > 2 Corinthians 5:21

As we become part of God's kingdom with this imputed righteousness, God expects us to live our lives according to the righteousness of Jesus in us, to be instructed by the word of God, and guided by the Holy Spirit every step of the way.

If the Holy Spirit is leading you to repent and receive Jesus in your life as your Lord and Savior, you can use this prayer as a pattern to speak your heart to the Lord:

Prayer of Repentance

> Heavenly Father, I come before you with a broken and contrite heart. I have sinned and lived my life thoughtlessly. I followed my own way instead of yours.
>
> Forgive me Father, I repent of all pride and rebellion. Forgive me for loving and pursuing the things of this world over you. Forgive me for bowing down to graven images or other material idols in this world. Forgive me for living a self-directed life.
>
> I surrender my life and will to Christ. I receive Jesus in my life not only as Lord and Savior but also as Shepherd to guide me in the path you have prepared for me beforehand.
>
> Thank you Father for not abandoning us by ourselves. Thank you for sending the Lord Jesus to us. Now I belong to Jesus who gave his life to ransom my soul. Lord, thank you for bringing me into the family of God and giving me eternal life. From now on help me to follow you and live my life to the glory of God. Amen.

POST-SCRIPT
Epilogue

- What do you think happened to Lost, the featured character in our story?
- Did Lost survive the plane crash? If she died, where could she be? Is she in heaven or separated from God forever in hell? If she escaped death from that fatal accident, could she have cried out to the Lord to save her? How would you like the story of Lost to end?
- What about you? What's the story as relates to your standing before God? What do you think God sees in you? Does he see Jesus in you? How would you like your own story to end?

SOMETHING TO CONSIDER

Since we started this book with a story, let's look at one last which happened to be a true insightful story from the bible—the story of Cain and Abel in the book of Genesis.

Cain and Abel were brothers, sons of Adam and Eve. Cain was older and he worked the ground as a farmer. Abel worked as a shepherd of flocks. When the time came to present a worship offering to God, Cain and Abel brought to the Lord their respective gifts.

Epilogue

In the course of time, Cain presented some of the land's produce as an offering to the Lord. Abel also presented an offering—some of the firstborn of his flock and their fat portions. The Lord had regard for Abel and his offering, but he did not have regard for Cain's. Cain was furious and became disheartened (Genesis 4:3–5).

"The Lord said to Cain, 'Why are you angry, and why has your face fallen? If you do well, will you not be accepted? And if you do not do well, sin is crouching at the door. Its desire is contrary to you, but you must rule over it'" (Genesis 4:6–7).

Why did God not accept Cain and his offering? Was there something wrong about his offering of the fruit of the ground which he toiled over time? What was wrong with Cain?

The Lord saw something that was not right with Cain's heart attitude, hence his offering was rejected. Cain worshipped God according to his own way, there is no mention that he gave of the first fruits of his crop as offering to the Lord (v3). This first-fruit offering is a requirement by God from his people, upon which God assured his blessing on their subsequent harvest (Proverbs 3:9–10). Put God first and all other things shall be added unto us. This is one way to test the heart of a true believer toward God.

It wasn't just what Cain offered that was lacking, God was also displeased in how Cain offered an external form of worship. Cain presented his gift before God without examining and addressing the rebellion and pride that were lurking in his heart. He was just going through the motions, extending his offering by hand but his heart was not in it. God saw through this, and gave Cain a chance to reflect, repent, and rule over the sin that was crouching within. But Cain's heart was hardened; he refused to listen to God. Cain's lack of regard for God left him unable or even unwilling to arrest the sin that was creeping in his heart; sin grieves God and separates man from him. Cain's story ended tragically as he chose to ignore God's counsel, succumbed to the evil that gripped him, and ended up killing his brother Abel. "Talk no more so very proudly, let not arrogance come from your mouth; for the Lord is a God of knowledge, and by him actions are weighed" (1 Samuel 2:3).

Why did God accept Abel and his offering? Abel presented to God his honorary gift—the best portions of the firstborn lambs

Epilogue

from his flock (v4). Abel's offering was sanctified by his faith in God. The gift that Abel presented was the product of a heart and will that put God first, trusted in him, and sought to obey him. Abel came to worship God whom he loved and knew. It was on account of Abel's faith that God was pleased and commended him as righteous. We know this to be true because Hebrews 11:4 says so, "By faith Abel offered to God a more acceptable sacrifice than Cain, through which he was commended as righteous, God commending him by accepting his gifts. And through his faith, though he died, he still speaks."

God is not moved by the material form of any offering made unto him; instead, God weighs the heart attitude of the offeror. Good deeds glorify God and are acceptable to him if they are offered out of hands and hearts that are pardoned, reconciled, and submitted in faith to him—by men and women who know Christ and do things out of the overflow of their love for him. Our worship, anything that we offer unto God, cannot be detached from the affections that we nurture within. The mind and heart that please God are marked by a desire to honor him, not out of a sense of duty or obligation, but out of a life that loves Christ and strives to obey him.

How about you? Will God find your life offering acceptable like Abel, or will he reject it like Cain? Have you asked God to wash and cleanse your sins by the shed blood of Christ? Is the posture of your heart bowed in submission to him? May we never rest until we know in absolute certainty that our hearts and will are set right before the Lord, as proven by the word of God.

Nothing is more important than ensuring that our life, body, and soul belong to Christ; that our eternal salvation is secured not by our own workings but in Christ's own strength, sufficiency, and unchangeable nature.

> "And this is the testimony: that God has given us eternal life, and this life is in His Son. He who has the Son has life; he who does not have the Son of God does not have life. These things I have written to you who believe in the name of the Son of God, that you may know that you have eternal life, and that you may continue to believe in the name of the Son of God."
>
> 1 John 5:11–13 (NKJV)

Bibliography

Chapman, Paul. "4 Types of Love (Agape, Phileo and . . .)." www.PaulEChapman.com. August 3, 2019. https://paulechapman.com/2019/08/03/4-types-of-love-agape-phileo-and/.

Chester, Tim. *An Ocean of Grace; A Journey to Easter with Great Voices from the Past.* The Fifth Week of Lent, Friday - Medicine for the Soul. UK: The Good Book Company, 2021.

Cook, Beckett. "How to Love Your LGBT Neighbor During Pride Month (and Every Month)." June 8, 2021. Copyright © 2021 Becket Cook. All rights reserved. https://www.boundless.org/blog/how-to-love-your-lgbt-neighbor-during-pride-month-and-every-month/.

Focus on the Family. "Biblical Perspective on Homosexuality and Same-Sex Marriage." Copyright © 2022, Focus on the Family. https://www.focusonthefamily.com/family-qa/biblical-perspective-on-homosexuality-and-same-sex-marriage/.

Got Questions Ministries. "Who were the Pharisees?" January 4, 2022. https://www.gotquestions.org/Pharisees.html.

Pearcey, Nancy. *Love Thy Body: Answering Hard Questions about Life and Sexuality.* Baker, a division of Baker Publishing Group, 2018.

Pratney, Winkie A. (Revised Edition, 1983). *Youth Aflame: A Manual for Discipleship.* Copyright © 1970, 1983. Used by permission of Bethany House, Minneapolis, Minnesota 55438. www.bethanyhouse.com.

Rushing, Richard, ed. *Voices from the Past, Volume 2.* Pennsylvania, USA: The Banner of Truth Trust, 2019.

Ryken, Phil. *Loving Jesus More.* Wheaton, Illinois: Crossway. Used by permission of Crossway, a publishing ministry of Good News, Wheaton, IL 60187, 2014. www.crossway.org.

Ryle, J.C. *Daily Readings from all four Gospels. For morning and evening.* Welwyn Garden City, UK: Evangelical, 2015.

Sawyer, Nathan. "A Re-Preaching of the Historic Sermon by Gilbert Tennent. Ezekiel 33:11 | Historic Sermon: Total Depravity - The Wretched State of the Unconverted." Grace Church, Memphis, TN. December 29, 2019.

Bibliography

https://www.gracechurchmemphis.com/sermons/total-depravity-the-wretched-state-of-the-unconverted.

Snyder, John. "Behold Your God: The Weight of Majesty." Media Gratiae: Consecrated, Lord, to Thee. March 30, 2021. https://www.mediagratiae.org/blog/consecrated-lord-to-thee.

Snyder, John and Chuck Baggett. "Total Depravity." Media Gratiae: The Whole Counsel. March 11, 2021. https://www.mediagratiae.org/blog/total-depravity.

Tozer, A.W. "The purpose of good works isn't to change or save us; rather, it's the demonstration of the change within us." AZQuotes.com. Wind and Fly LTD, 2022. https://www.azquotes.com/quote/907820.

Made in the USA
Las Vegas, NV
12 February 2023

67388533R00095